latest edn
1/v ST

on
fil

Drw

KU-002-520

The Team Guide to Communication

John Middleton

Adviser in General Practice
University of Leicester

Radcliffe Medical Press

© 2000 John Middleton

Radcliffe Medical Press Ltd
18 Marcham Road, Abingdon, Oxon OX14 1AA

All rights reserved. No part of this publication may be reproduced, stored in a retrieval system or transmitted, in any form or by any means, electronic, mechanical, photocopying, recording or otherwise without the prior permission of the copyright owner.

British Library Cataloguing in Publication Data

A catalogue record for this book is available from the British Library.

ISBN 1 85775 411 5

CROYDON COLLEGE
LIBRARY

COPY 05 2 S804

CLASS 616 MID

Typeset by Multiplex Medway Ltd., Walderslade, Kent
Printed and bound by TJ International Ltd., Padstow, Cornwall

Contents

Preface

Nothing is more important for the health professional than the ability to communicate with other people. Between professional and client, learner and teacher, or in groups, the skills of communication are absolutely vital.

I've spent my professional life as a doctor in a group practice, seeing patients, training young doctors and teaching the teachers. In all of these situations, whether one to one or in groups, I've found that communication works better if people listen to and respect each other. What's more, the attitude of wanting to do this goes a long way towards achieving a good result. We can all learn to release the skills that are already within us.

So, it's all quite simple and you don't need to read this book – but don't go away just yet! Theories about communication often seem anything but simple. The jargon can be off-putting, and I can't promise you that this book is free from it. However, I have found that using the agenda or 'face' model keeps me in touch with the essential simplicity which I believe is at the heart of successful communication. It helps me not to lose sight of the importance of mutual respect for one another's point of view, amidst the forest of tasks and concepts that has grown up in the field of communication. The simplicity of the model also enables it to be used in a wide variety of situations, where it seems to act as a unifying principle. Whether or not you agree with this, there are other models you will meet on the way. Use or discard them as you wish!

All books should really carry a disclaimer of the 'don't try this at home' variety. I can only go on my own experience and what I have heard about that of others. There is a relative scarcity of hard evidence in the field of education. I believe that what I am suggesting will help, but don't blame me if it doesn't! You might have to keep trying, or adapt the approach to your own personality and situation.

I am quite sure that you can't learn communication skills from a book, which might seem a strange thing to say in the preface of one on the subject. Repeated practice and feedback are the real keys to improving any kind of skill. I hope that the exercises suggested in this book will be a useful stimulus, that other parts will help you to reflect on the skills, and that you will learn to develop those skills that you already have.

Multiprofessional education is likely to increase in importance with the advent of primary care groups and clinical governance. The subject of communication, at different levels and in different situations, is one of the main candidates for acting as a bridge between professional groups in healthcare teams. Teamwork and communication are inextricably linked. I am only too aware that the medical voices and contexts predominate in this book. Although I try to listen to other members of the team. I cannot help being a doctor and therefore being able to write best about what I know. The advantage of being a one-man band is that the book could be written within a reasonable time-scale. However, if there are future editions, I would like to include contributions from my other colleagues.

This book is not intended to represent an academic approach to communication, although some theory and references have been inescapable. I have tried to write as if I was addressing another person, in an attempt to make the material more accessible. One-way communication like this is not in the spirit of the book, I know. If I met you at a social event, and you found me irritating, I like to think that I would pick up the vibes and back off. Here in my garret I am quite isolated from feedback. I mean no offence, and I only wish to help.

My final disclaimer is that none of the characters in this book are based intentionally on real individuals. I know that they are merely figments of my imagination (so I'm not sectionable yet). In fact, I started hearing the voices in Chapter 2, and they just grew from there. If you don't find them amusing, try ignoring them. I did, but they wouldn't go away.

John Middleton
May 2000

Acknowledgements

I would like to thank all those whose work I have quoted, unintentionally misquoted, reproduced and – hopefully – acknowledged in the text. To a very great extent there is nothing new in the field of communication. Everything has already been said. It's just the way I tell 'em.

I would also like to thank my friends and colleagues in the practice team. They are a great bunch of people, and I want you to know that.

Last but not least, thanks to my wife and family for putting up with my lack of communication, and my hogging the computer for the last few months.

Croydon College
Library & Learning Centre

Issue Summary

Borrower: Miss Patricia Greenidge
Id: 6165**
Date: 21/11/2018 10:49

Loaned today

Item: 38017001225804
Title: The team guide to communication
Due back: **12/12/2018**

Thank you for using self service

To
Henry and Nora,
Erica,
Anthony and Rachael

CHAPTER ONE

A tale of two neighbours
AN INTRODUCTION TO THE 'FACE' MODEL

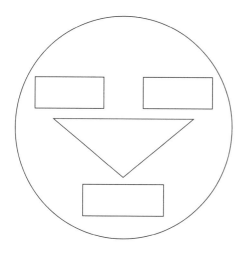

Figure 1.1

In the beginning was the one-to-one. That is where all the trouble started – Adam and Eve, patients, doctors, nurses, social workers and clients, to name but a few. Jean-Paul Sartre said that hell is the existence of other people.

THINK BOX

People complain about health workers.

What do they complain about?

What are the most common complaints?

Have you had a patient/client complain about you? (Come on, be honest.)

How does it make you feel? (That complaints are jewels?)

What has made *you* want to complain as a patient/client? (You didn't like their attitude; they didn't listen, or didn't value what you had to say – am I right? These are common complaints which emerge in user surveys. Have you any additions or variations on the themes?)

So what is happening, in the one-to-one interaction, to cause all this trouble? It can be made very complicated – with lots of models (and I don't mean Page Three).[1-5] Or it can be simple. Which would you prefer?

Let's stay simple for now. Otherwise you can skip ahead.

Think of a meeting between two people. Let's call them Donald and Liam, for the sake of argument, and let's say they are neighbours.

Donald has a sycamore tree which overhangs Liam's drive. Every autumn, Liam has to sweep up the leaves and every year the tree grows bigger. Donald loves trees. Liam has already removed all the trees in his own garden.

THINK BOX

What does Liam want to say to Donald?

What are Liam's ideas about the subject?

Why does he think those things?

What will Donald think that Liam really means?

How does Liam think that Donald will interpret what he has to say?

What does Donald think about what Liam will be thinking about his (Donald's) reaction?

Are you dizzy yet?

I said it would be simple. All I'm trying to show is the enormous potential for misunderstanding. Laing talks about *knots* and *metaperspectives*.[6] Yeah, man.

THINK BOX

What about Donald?

What does he want to say to Liam?

What are his ideas on the subject?

Why does he think those things?

What does Liam think Donald really means?

Etc.

But this is not the only problem that they need to discuss. What about Liam's noisy children, the neighbourhood-watch scheme, and the millennium party?
And while we're here, what about...?

I won't go on, but do you get the point? Both Liam and Donald arrive at their meeting with a load of baggage (issues, ideas and reasoning). I call each pile of baggage an *agenda*. Okay, I know it's jargon, but it's in the model.

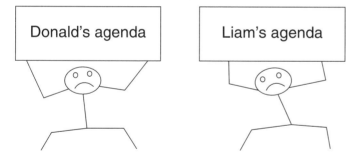

Figure 1.2

What they need from their meeting is some kind of plan which is acceptable to both. I know it doesn't always work out that way with neighbours. (And what about consultations with nurses, doctors or other health professionals?)

I'm sure you have your own ideas about how to manage trees, gardens, children, dogs, etc. Let's just pretend that the following is a mutually acceptable plan.

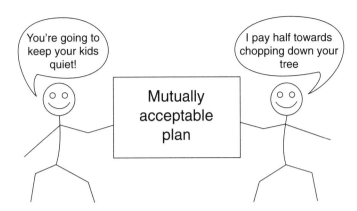

Figure 1.3

How did they get there? Never mind whether or not you think it will work – that's the subject of this book. It concerns communication skills. Here they are.

Figure 1.4

Now let's assemble the *agenda* model.

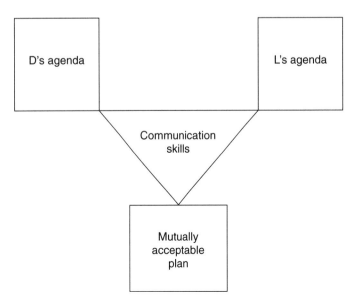

Figure 1.5

We all know what agendas are, don't we? Even so, the word has the flavour of jargon.

Some people prefer to call this model the *face*. Why? Because it has two eyes, a nose and a mouth.

Simple models are the most useful kind, in my opinion, because you can easily see what is happening, and that also makes it easy to remember.

This model applies to any form of communication between people. Not just Liam and Donald, but A and B and anyone else you can think of (including health professionals and each other, or their clients/patients).

The model is dynamic. The agendas are forces which are often unequal and not in harmony. Everything flows from them, or at least from the parts which are able to be expressed.

Liam and Donald's mutually agreed plan resulted from successful sharing of their agendas, which was achieved by the exercise of communication skills.

The tale of the social worker

So much for the tale of two neighbours.

And who *is* my neighbour? Let me remind you of the story in the Bible (Luke 11: 29 – 36), in which the Samaritan used his position of relative power and influence to improve the health of a man who had been left for dead. (Jesus neatly reversed the question: 'Which...was neighbour unto him that fell among thieves?')

THINK BOX

Here's one for the creative thinkers out there.

What was the victim's agenda?

What was the Samaritan's agenda?

Did the Samaritan subordinate his own agenda to the needs of the victim?

It seems to me that the health professional's role is rather like this – to be a neighbour to the sick – to facilitate the process for the person in need of their services.

EXERCISE

Think of a recent interaction with a client/patient when you were aware of your own personal agenda.

How did you deal with that awareness?

Did you share any of that personal agenda with the client/patient?

How did you come to that decision?

How does this relate to *being a professional?*

There's something here about distance between a professional and client, isn't there? Perhaps it's easier in hospital practice, but out here in primary care? You get to know people quite well, don't you? Have you actually shed tears? We all feel like that sometimes.

There's something about power as well.

THINK BOX

Generally speaking, in the interaction between yourself and a patient/client, who has the most power?

Why is that?

Do you think that the power balance has changed or is changing?

Why?

Is that a good thing?

Is the balance of power very different in interactions with other types of primary care professional?

You may have heard the story of the doctor who ordered a patient with back pain to lie down flat and *not move a muscle.*

Some months later, a relative telephoned to ask if it was okay for the patient to sit up yet.

It is an old story, and I don't suppose for a minute that it is true.

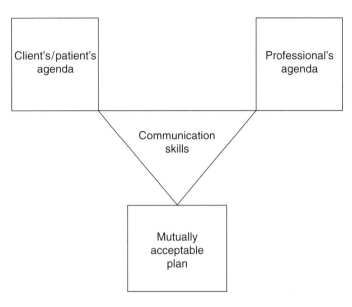

Figure 1.6

EXERCISE

Think of a recent interview/consultation with a client/patient.

What did you think was the client's/patient's agenda?

What was on your agenda? (Think around it as widely as possible.)

What was the outcome?

What were the problems with the interaction?

What skills were needed?

Perhaps the health professional should make identification of the client's/patient's agenda their first priority.

THINK BOX

To what extent do you subordinate the rest of your professional agenda to that of the client/patient?

To what extent are you the agent of the client/patient?

If you have power, do you use it for the good of the individual client/patient?

Power is not always an entirely benign influence, is it?

The tale of the salesman

Once upon a time, Fred, a middle-aged man with a wife and two children, went to buy a new small family car. The salesman was very affable, and knew a great deal about cars and what suited different people. He seemed very interested in Fred's family, and even asked where they went for their holidays. He seemed a little surprised that Fred was considering such a small car, in view of the position he had reached. Fred's wife had thought for a long time that he didn't push himself forward enough, otherwise he might have achieved more.

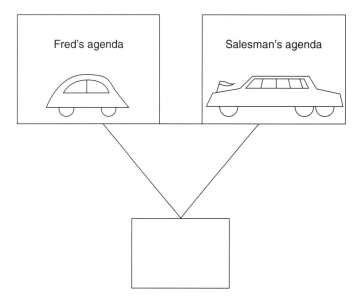

Figure 1.7

THINK BOX

If you've never bought a new car, think of a similar situation, in which someone was trying to sell you something.

Did the salesperson attempt to discover your agenda?

If so, did they try to use part of your agenda to further their sales pitch?

Did it work?

---

1   Trust me, I'm a salesman.
2   Trust me, I'm a doctor.
3   Trust me, I'm a nurse.

4   Trust me, I'm a health visitor.
5   Trust me, I'm a social worker.
6   Trust me, I'm a manager.

Circle the statement which seems to you to be most true.

I bet you didn't circle number one.

Yes, you can trust the primary healthcare team, can't you? They have your best interests, not their own, at heart. But what about health promotion? Isn't that like salesmanship? And what about target payments? What about the mutually acceptable plan at the end of the consultation? If you haven't sold the plan, it may not be carried out.

Trust is something you must have, though, if you want to find out and work with the patient's or client's agenda. And if they see your plan as irrelevant to their agenda, they'll sabotage it!

Learners and teachers

EXERCISE

Think of a situation in your professional education where you were the learner.

What was your agenda?

What seemed to be the teacher's agenda?

What were the problems?

What skills were needed?

Conversely, consider a situation where you have been a teacher.

What was the learner's agenda?

What was your agenda?

What were the problems?

What skills were needed?

THINK BOX

Can you think of some more parallels between teaching/learning, consulting/interviewing and selling?

Well, go on then, what are the differences?

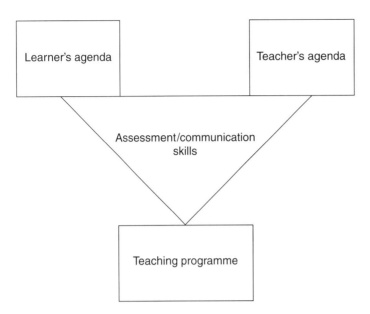

Figure 1.8

We'll come back to the details later in this book.

What about groups?

First, let us consider a group of three.

EXERCISE

Think of a consultation/interview with a patient/client in which a third party was present.

How did the presence of a third person change what happened?

What problems arose?

What skills were needed?

In a consultation with a patient/client and a relative, there are three agendas.

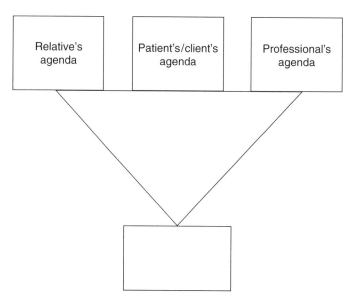

Figure 1.9

The balance of power is more complicated.

The professional must discover the agenda of the relative as well as that of the patient/client.

Sometimes a third party may have a powerful influence on proceedings even in their absence.

Can you think of an instance of this, from your own practice?

EXERCISE

What groups are you in?

What are your roles in those groups?

What problems have you noticed?

What skills were needed?

Extending the agenda model to a larger group:

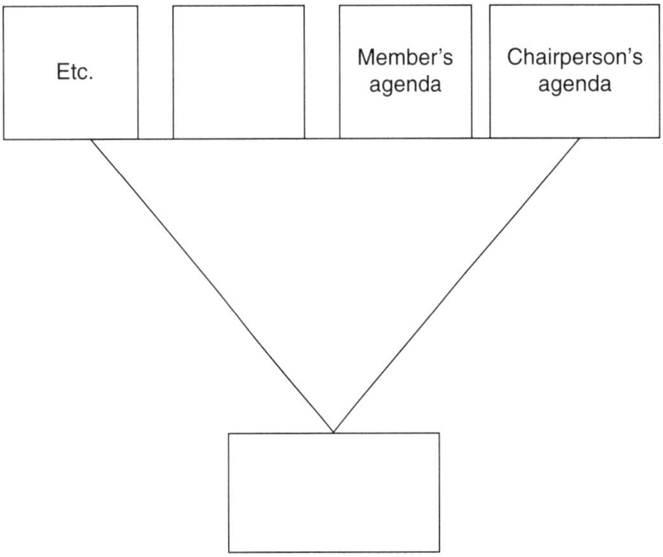

Figure 1.10

In groups, the opportunities for multiple agendas, power balances and plain dysfunction are multiplied. Perhaps it is not surprising that there is so much trouble (I know, I know – your groups are all wonderful – come and be a tutor on my course).

The agenda/'face' model

So now you're convinced, aren't you? The agenda model applies to all forms of interpersonal communication, whether one-to-one or in groups.

A successful outcome (hence the smiley face), in terms of a mutually agreed plan, depends on each party understanding something of the standpoint (agenda) of the other.

Reaching that point depends on the application of appropriate communication skills which, incidentally, we all possess. Yes! Even the least socially able of us have these skills.

As you work through this book, you will be able to reflect on your own strengths and weaknesses. Play to your strengths!

Those are the principles of the model, and you have seen how it relates to negotiations between neighbours, consultations/interviews between clients/patients and health professionals, salesmanship, teaching/learning and groups. You have even had some old-time religion. Politics will come later.

Here's the smiley face.

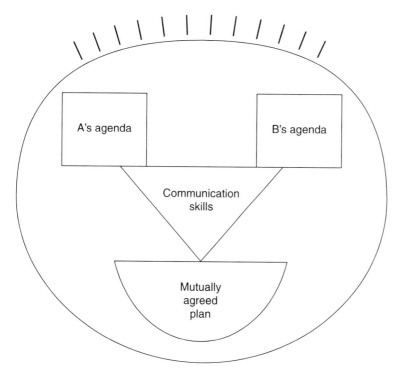

Figure 1.11

I'm sure you want to get on and find out how to make those communication skills work for you as a health professional. And that's just what we're going to do, but don't forget the agendas.

May the *face* be with you.

CHAPTER TWO

Is anyone there?
PROBLEMS IN THE CONSULTATION

Well, is there? I mean intelligent life – out there in the galaxy?

'No. Otherwise they would have got a message to us by now' says Donald.

'But have we developed the right instruments? Are we really listening?' says Liam.

Just answer the question!

Here is a vignette.

Scene: a middle-aged male doctor's consulting-room in a suburban practice. Pictures of the doctor's family and his diplomas adorn the walls. The shelves are full of old medical textbooks. The patient is a young female art student.

Kerry-Ann: 'Doctor, my throat is really really sore.'

Dr Strait: 'Mmm...'.

Kerry-Ann: 'And I feel really really hot.'

Dr Strait: 'How long for?'

Kerry-Ann: 'What?'

Dr Strait: 'How long have you had your sore throat?'

Kerry-Ann: 'Quite a while.'

Dr Strait: 'How long is "quite a while"?'

Kerry-Ann: 'I'm not really sure.'

Dr Strait: 'Well, has it been days, weeks, months, years?'

Kerry-Ann: 'Well I don't know...it came on gradually...that's why I've come.'

Dr Strait: 'I see... Does anything make that sore throat worse...or better?'

Kerry-Ann: 'No, I haven't taken anything. I thought I'd come and see you.'

Dr Strait: 'Anything else?'

Kerry-Ann: 'What do you mean?'

Dr Strait: 'Any other pains or aches anywhere?'

Kerry-Ann: 'Nothing as bad as this.'

The doctor looks in the patient's mouth with a torch.

Dr Strait: 'Hmm... Looks a bit red, I suppose.'

THINK BOX

Try to imagine the thoughts of the doctor and patient after each line of the above dialogue.

What do you think might be the significance of the expression 'really really' (as in 'my throat is really really sore')?

What do you think the patient wants, and why? You could suggest several possibilities.

What might have happened next?

EXERCISE

Suppose that the health professional in that scenario was not a doctor, but (say) a nurse. Would you have to rewrite the dialogue?

Go on, try it.

What are the differences, if any?

If there are differences, can you give reasons for them?

Perhaps you didn't think much of this doctor? Well, I'll come clean – it was me.

At least, it might have been, on a Monday morning. It might have been many other doctors, too – I've seen them on video.

Nurses, of course, don't behave like that, do they? What *is* it about doctors that stops them listening?

People complain about it at parties (before they realise that I'm a doctor). ('They don't listen to you. You can't tell them anything.')

Were the people who became doctors always like that? Was it perhaps the training? If other health professionals are doing better, shouldn't doctors be learning from them?

I'm not trying to antagonise my colleagues. Honestly!

No, there are good reasons why doctors have difficulties with communication. I think it's partly the pressure (especially time), and partly some of the aspects of medical training.

'Clinical method' is taught to medical students, and it is often followed slavishly by the least experienced, but it is ingrained in all doctors, believe me.

In the hands of the novice, it is a tool of interrogation. I say 'in the hands of a novice' because interrogation, in the negative sense, is not an essential part of the method. Indeed, I well remember some of the experienced teachers advising us to stop asking so many questions:

'Listen to the patients – they are telling you the diagnosis.'

All very well if you have half an hour to spare, some of us might say. And that is partly the problem. Under pressure, there is a tendency to regress to an earlier stage of development, according to Erickson, that is.[1] Why else do wounded soldiers call for their mothers?

Clinical method

- History of the presenting complaint(s).
- System review (to trawl for anything else not presented).
- Examination.
- Investigation.
- Diagnosis.
- Treatment.

Even now, I can still hear my teachers say, 'The three most important things are the diagnosis, the diagnosis, and the diagnosis!'

It is quite logical, as clinical method is logical. Obviously, you must have the right diagnosis to get the right treatment. Right?

Well, it depends on how important you think treatment is, out here in primary care. What is treatment anyway? (No, I'm not going to become all philosophical. At least I didn't ask 'what is truth?' So you don't have to tear your clothes.) Actually, what does the patient want? Is it penicillin, or a note for college, or is the sore throat the entry ticket so that she can unload some other problem?

Don't get me wrong. Doctors have to be able to make an accurate diagnosis *where appropriate*. They have to be competent in using clinical method, but that does not mean firing questions, when you can obtain the information some other way – by listening, actually. Save the questions if there are gaps you really have to fill. That applies not just to clinical method, but to communication across the board. Away with the system review (as Hoffbrand said).[2]

Ask a silly question and you get a silly answer. If your questions seem irrelevant to the client/patient, they won't pay proper attention to them, and their answers won't be very useful. So why not save your breath?

Listen to the client/patient – they are telling you something really really important.

It is not necessarily the diagnosis, but it is certainly important to them. That is why you have to understand it.

Why have they come? It is a simple enough question, but it is one which doctors often fail to answer, according to research.[3,4]

Byrne and Long described a spectrum of doctor behaviour in the consultation, ranging from 'doctor-centred' (rooted in the paternalistic approach, clinical method and the biomedical perspective) to 'patient-centred' (tending towards power-sharing, joint decision-making and a perspective including the social–psychological sphere). They found very little flexibility in the style of individual doctors.

Eric Berne's parent/adult/child model illustrates how these two styles of doctor behaviour work.[5] The theory is that each of us has the capacity to communicate in any of the three modes, according to the situation, or our own personal inclinations.

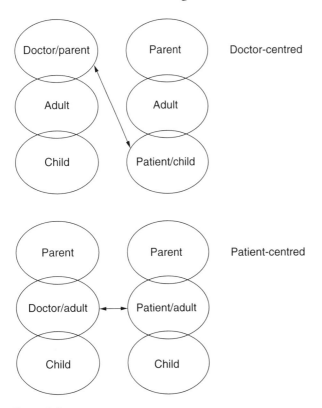

Figure 2.1

Don't you just love being told what to do by an authority figure?

Take these tablets and you'll get better.

People used to like it more than they seem to do now. What exactly are these tablets? What are the side-effects? Are there any alternatives? When I was a GP trainee, only teachers used to ask these types of questions. Sorry, dear (my wife's a teacher – so am I, come to think of it).

These ways of interacting seem to work well so long as each participant accepts their role. Meanwhile, however, the world has been changing. Patients and clients have different expectations and more knowledge. Have we adapted sufficiently to the shift in the balance of power? Or is it a case of 'stop the world, we'd like to stay put'?

Like doctors, patients and clients exhibit a wide spectrum of behaviours, ranging from the compliant (ask no questions and do as you're told) to the assertive (using their mobile phones for another opinion during the consultation).

Do I exaggerate? Not much.

Returning to dear old Byrne and Long, using audio-tapes they constructed a series of events in the consultation between doctor and patient.[3] This was one of the earliest models of the consultation, and it appears to be in widespread use by GP trainers today. This is probably because the sequence of events remains highly relevant, and therefore easy to remember 'on the job'.

It was, after all, not so much a model as a description of the events on the tapes, in order of appearance. I shall attempt to paraphrase it below.

1   Establish a relationship.
2   Discover the reasons for attendance.
3   Conduct an examination (including verbal examination).
4   Consider the problem.
5   Make a plan.
6   Close.

Byrne and Long[3] found that item 2 was where the problems most often arose – then everything else just fell apart.

Why didn't the doctors just ask the patients straight out what they wanted? Were they perhaps afraid of opening Pandora's box? To me, that sounds like an exciting prospect, but I'd like more than 5 or 6 minutes to deal with the contents, thank you very much. So, as it's Monday morning, let's put the lid back on for now, shall we?

THINK BOX

Whether or not you are a doctor, how relevant is Byrne and Long's model to your one-to-one interactions with patients or clients today?

Is there anything you would like to add?

Or to subtract?

Are most of your problems related to item 2 in the sequence?

If not, what *are* your most frequent problems?

Why?

EXERCISE

Record some of your one-to-one interactions with clients/patients on audio or (preferably) video tape.

Note: You will need written informed consent to do this (see Appendix 1).

How did you behave (for example, in terms of parent/adult/child)?

How did your client or patient behave?

Did they give you a hard time?

Were Byrne and Long at all useful?

Looking back at the interactions, what would you most like help with?

No matter how loudly you shout, I can't hear your replies to these questions. However, I can tell you the most frequent problem that my GP registrars identified, having watched their own video tapes.

We want to learn how to do the explanation like you do, they said. When you tell them, the patients listen. When we try it, they keep interrupting. So I watched the tapes with them. It looked as if the registrars were explaining something that didn't interest the patients. I suggested that they found something to talk about that *did* interest the patients, and this worked. That takes us back to Byrne and Long's item 2.

How does that relate to your experience?

So far, most of this discussion has been about doctors and patients. What about other healthcare professionals?

For example, to what extent do you think the roles of doctor and nurse are converging? What about nurse practitioners? Is it mainly a matter of time constraints? After all, 10 minutes is quite generous for a doctor's consultation, and pretty mean for most other healthcare professionals. However, practice nurses are now increasingly finding their time being constrained. Are you behaving more like doctors as a result?

Or is it mainly about different training, traditions and responsibilities? GPs feel that almost any kind of problem – medical or not – may be presented to them. Is that becoming true for practice nurses, and was it always true for health visitors?

District nurses use check-lists when they are making new patient assessments. The old hands tell me that they learn to discard the check-lists when the situation demands it. The less experienced ones tend to get the structure round their necks (now that sounds familiar).

However, they allocate one hour for new patient assessments. That is where we seem to be inhabiting different planets. Despite this, our nurses tell me that they still get 'by-the-way syndrome' – just when you think you've tied everything up, the patient comes out with the real problem. That must be really sickening after 59 minutes of following a check-list (so much for silly questions).

Listen, anyone who has ears (Matthew 13: 43).

So much to do, so little time!

That's what my wife says.

That's what my partners say.

That's what my patients say (at least, those with jobs).

Value for money was the song of the 1990s – it means one person doing two people's jobs.

Crank up the stress to increase productivity. It works, but beyond a certain critical point the elasticity is lost and the mechanism is permanently damaged, resulting in reduced performance.

As far as I remember from 'O'-level physics, when applied to metal springs, this is called hysteresis. When applied to people, 'hysteria' might be nearer the mark. The reduced performance is called 'burnout'. In a caring profession, this is particularly unfortunate, don't you think?

I'm very sorry, all of the doctors are out or off sick, but Sister Brasstoff can squeeze you in.

The above game (moaning about the situation we're in) is called 'ain't it awful?' (see Eric Berne's book),[5] and is a favourite of health professionals.

My belief is that eventually some important person will realise that overstressed carers are not good value for patients, but perhaps I am too much of an optimist. Anyway, unless you are planning a career in politics, there is not much you can do about it.

Cheer up! We'll cope, we always do – there are ways. Read on.

There are too many tasks, but where do they all come from? Some come from outside, often from a great height. Perhaps others are self-imposed.

Returning to the medical consultation, doctors are trained to make diagnoses, and they have had to learn all types of check-lists and templates to help them to do this.

On old Olympus' towering top
A Finn and German viewed a hop.

That is the polite version of a mnemonic for the cranial nerves.

So when you (as a patient) complain to the doctor about feeling tired, his or her brain could be going into overdrive, generating almost endless possible explanations for this very common problem.

Learning to use 'clinical method' partly involves internalising sequences of questions, such as 'how long for?', 'what makes it better/worse?' etc. (Look back at the vignette with Dr Strait.)

Doctors also have acronyms for remembering all of the possible jobs they might have to do in the consultation.

RAPRIOP

Sounds painful, doesn't it? Actually, it stands for:

- reassure/explain
- advice
- prescription
- referral
- investigation
- observation/follow-up
- prevention.

Then there were new improved models of the consultation that followed on from Byrne and Long.

First off the blocks was one from Stott and Davis, who thought that the full potential of the consultation was not being realised, and that *doctors should be doing more:*[6]

1   management of presenting problems
2   management of continuing problems
3   modification of health-seeking behaviour
4   opportunistic health promotion.

You have to remember that this was an era when some doctors were being criticised for spending time on the golf course. I can remember eating lunch – at home!

Items 2, 3 and 4 seem like new tasks – at least I can't find them in Byrne and Long. The new idea is to look beyond the presenting problem. For example, the patient may have hypertension or be an alcohol abuser, and present with an unrelated problem such as earache. Here is an opportunity to check their blood pressure, advise about safe drinking and make sure that appropriate use of the appointment system is understood. The four points could be summarised on the back of your hand in biro, so here is a framework that can be used 'on the hoof' in the middle of the consultation.

Sibelius said that his symphonies gave you cold water, just like Byrne and Long when you think about it. All of a sudden, with Stott and Davis, you're in Mahler territory – the whole of human life is there. The only problem is that it all sounds a little managerial, don't you think? *Management* of presenting problems and *management* of continuing problems – Beethoven conducted by Herbert von Karajan perhaps? How about modification of concert-going behaviour? You *will not* cough during the quiet bits.

Enter a friendly social psychologist (I'm told they can make dogs salivate in teams) called David Pendleton, whose team came up with a social skills model.[7] According to the theory, discrete components of human behaviour can be described and taught using a technique of immediate feedback, rather as specific skills can be taught and practised when learning to drive a car. The technique is known as *microteaching*. Pendleton and his colleagues identified seven tasks for the doctor.[7]

1   To define the reason for the patient's attendance, including:
    • the nature and history of the problems
    • their aetiology
    • the patient's ideas, concerns and expectations
    • the effects of the problems.
2   To consider other problems:
    • continuing problems
    • at-risk factors.
3   To choose with the patient an appropriate action for each problem.
4   To achieve a shared understanding of the problems with the patient.
5   To involve the patient in the management of their case, and to involve them in acceptance of appropriate responsibility for it.
6   To use time and resources appropriately.
7   To establish or maintain a relationship with the patient which helps in the achievement of other tasks.

Task 1, although highly differentiated with its four subdivisions, is equivalent to item 2 of Byrne and Long[3] or item 1 of Stott and Davis.[6] The effect is *expansion and greater prominence of the reasons for attendance.* Task 2 is roughly equivalent to items 2 and 4 of Stott and Davis.[6] Tasks 3 to 5 seem to overlap, and have a new emphasis on *sharing.* Task 6 brings another new concept of *time and resources.* The final task is equivalent to item 1 of Byrne and Long.[3]

Pendleton's list of tasks is arguably the most comprehensive one for the consultation, and the model has given rise to a rating scale and consultation mapping tool (*see* Chapter 9), based on the seven tasks. Pure Bach, I'd say – It's the Well-Tempered Klavier all over again.

Whereas the four categories in the model of Stott and Davis can be scribbled on the back of the hand, Roger Neighbour consciously uses the five digits of the hand to identify the five check-points in his model:[8]

1   connecting (thumb)
2   summarising (index finger)
3   handing over (middle finger)
4   housekeeping (ring finger)
5   safety-netting (little finger).

Neighbour's thumb is Byrne and Long item 2 (and equivalents) all over again. The index (what I am hearing is...) and middle fingers (giving responsibility to the patient) are probably absorbed in Pendleton's items 3 to 5. The ring *(am I ready to give full attention to the next patient?)* and little fingers *(have I missed anything? what are the indications for review?)* appear to denote new concepts.

Whilst Pendleton appears to be firmly rooted in the external perspective of the behavioural school of psychology, Neighbour is interested in the internal workings of the brain in relation to the learning of skills (which he calls inner consulting). If you like 'knight's move' associations, (anything from art to Chinese philosophy), you'll probably enjoy his writing. Such eclecticism reminds me of the different musical styles of Igor Stravinsky. Perhaps I'm just as bad (don't answer that).

THINK BOX

Take a moment or two to think how far the three newer models might be an advance on Byrne and Long.

Could you draw a composite model including the features of all four?

Reflect on the effects of these models on the doctor's agenda in the consultation.

How do these effects tally with the patient-centred language in the later models?

Because Byrne and Long's model was based on a description of what they observed, there are no 'ought to do's', only what happens. The later models are certainly prescriptive (for doctors), and those of Stott and Davis,[6] and Pendleton and colleagues[7] introduce forces outside the immediate consultation – such as health promotion and targets. Suddenly there are many gremlins lurking – the practice, the doctor's family, public health personnel, primary care groups, the government and, last but not least, 'Big Brother' in the form of our desktop computer screen.

With all of these new pressures, what about time (and resources, according to Pendleton)? Well, there's never enough of either.

That means conflict. That means rationing. Ouch! Where's the patient's agenda? It just got squeezed. No, it's all right – the government represents the patient. But what about the individual patients? What about them? They're unimportant, compared to the will of the majority.

It's difficult to argue with that. Everything has the feel of inevitability. 'Whichever way you vote, the government gets in' (that was a bit of graffiti I once read on a wall).

Still, inside the parochial confines of the consultation, it doesn't feel quite right. Stott himself later drew attention to the potential of the public health axis to destroy the essential function of the consultation as a dialogue between individuals. Noakes referred to the doctor as potentially becoming a 'double agent' for the state and the individual patient.[9]

THINK BOX

Is it only doctors, in the primary healthcare team, who might have divided loyalties?

Where else are those loyalties (or to whom else are you answerable)?

Think of your own role first.

Then try to understand the roles of others in the team.

Try asking them.

You might think that there were already enough medical models of the consultation (those I've described are not the only ones available), but one of the reasons why I made up my own model was to make it *less* medical and more general in application. This is because I have always seen the consultation as an interaction between two *people*, one of whom happens to be a health professional. I also wanted to get away from 'management', at least until near the end, and to focus more on what is in the minds of the participants – the *agendas* that they bring to the interaction. Finally, I wanted to show how the process is *dynamic*, involving potentially opposing forces which must be reconciled in order to produce a harmonious outcome, as suggested by Middleton.[10–12]

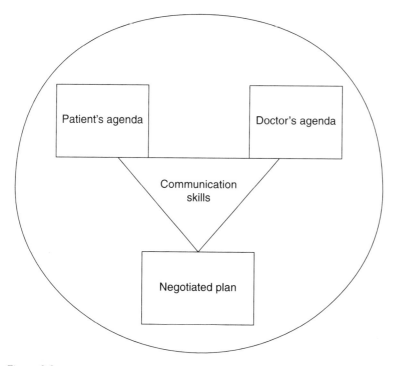

Figure 2.2

This is the *face* model, which was introduced in the first chapter.

However, at the moment, I'm only interested in the top right-hand box. What are all of these tasks and pressures doing to the poor old doctor's agenda (or perhaps the nurse's, health visitor's or practice manager's agendas)?

The doctor's (increasingly heavy) agenda

This consists of the following.

1   Discovering the patient's agenda.
2   Considering (and completing) the patient's database:
    *   continuing problems
    *   dormant problems
    *   risk factors.
3   Appropriate diagnosis and management of problems.
4   Private agenda:
    *   practice considerations
    *   external pressures
    *   personal agenda.

THINK BOX

Try to classify your own agenda in the one-to-one interaction (look back at your tape if it helps).

If you are not a doctor, what are the main differences from the above framework?

Why?

How does this relate to Dr Strait and his consultation with Kerry-Ann?

We have already seen how he was trying to define the problem (a sore throat) by asking a series of questions, and we left him attempting some examination (throat perhaps a little red), perhaps also pondering a diagnosis and suitable management (possibly a virus – symptomatic measures).

Kerry-Ann has a continuing problem of facial acne, for which she is already taking erythromycin. In the past, she has suffered from migraine which, although now dormant, might reactivate at any time, perhaps in response to the stress of moving away from her home district to go to college. She also smokes and consumes more than the recommended maximum quantity of alcohol for a female. So far Dr Strait knows none of this, as she has not yet had a new-patient check (for which there is an item-of-service payment). All this needs to be entered in the patient's database on the computer. The present consultation is one opportunity to discover and record such information. It may or may not relate to the present problem, but it is certainly relevant to the ability of Dr Strait's practice to achieve targets and higher health promotion bands. This will affect the doctor's income, in relation to other practices, and will also form part of the data collection for clinical governance by the local primary care group.

It is understandable if the good doctor is somewhat preoccupied by such considerations, don't you think? In fact, he only has 10 minutes (and then another 19 patients to go), so he's feeling anxious to polish off the presenting complaint in order to deal with some of his own agenda.

However, there is yet more. The appointment system is bursting at the seams. Over the last few years the list size has gradually increased, and the practice could do with an extra pair of hands, but the partners' family commitments make some of them reluctant to take a drop in income. In any case, they work in a restricted area, and might not be allowed to have an extra partner by the health authority. This has caused some friction between the doctors, and makes Dr Strait reluctant to have too many follow-up appointments. If Kerry-Ann doesn't get her sore throat sorted out now, it may be a week before she can have another appointment, unless she can convince the receptionist that it is an emergency, which is exactly what she had to do this morning!

Dr Strait is beginning to feel like a zombie. He's getting to the age when it seems more and more difficult to cope with the repeated imposition of changes in the health service, yet retirement is too far away to be a realistic option. He's taking work home in the evening and falling asleep with a large whisky in front of the television. His wife won't take much more.

Have you all got out your handkerchiefs? I thought not. It's every man or woman for themselves nowadays, isn't it?

We all have our problems. For the younger doctors, health visitors and all members of the primary healthcare team, they're not exactly the same, but they do affect us in our own ways. However, let us not waste sympathy on the health professionals – they have their trade unions to root for them. Our first concern must be for the patient, and I'm sure you've noticed that I put the patient's agenda first on the doctor's list of concerns. It was a worthy thought, but perhaps doomed to failure in view of the increasingly heavy agenda of the very professional who is supposed to be there to help them.

All is not lost. I'm painting a slightly gloomy picture in order to make a point. Let us look at what is on the patient's agenda (top left-hand box in Figure 2.2).

Before we do that, I want to try to see things from the viewpoint of other health professionals, particularly nurses. Although it might be true that practice nurses are carrying out consultations which increasingly resemble medical ones, the work of district nurses and health visitors is quite different. In any case, nurses are starting from a completely different perspective in their training.

The nursing model of Roper, Logan and Tierney[13]

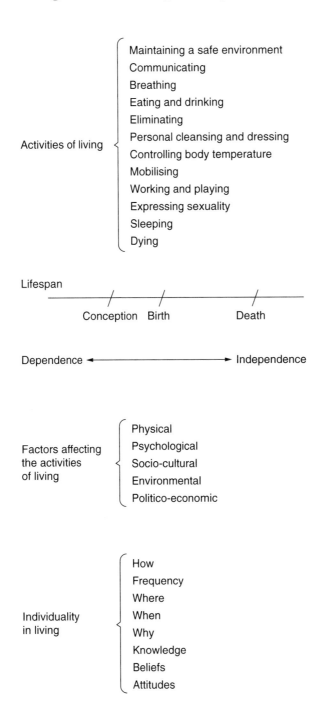

Figure 2.3

According to this model, patients carry out their activities of daily living against an unfolding series of events in the lifespan, with their associated positions on the dependence/independence continuum. Their expression is modified by various factors, such as the political or physical environment, and ultimately by the unique individuality of the patient.

Nurses see their function as being to assist the patient fully to perform these activities of living, within the limits for that individual in a particular context. This may sometimes involve taking account of a medical or other prescription, but it remains orientated to the needs of the whole patient.

EXERCISE

1   Write down the differences (and similarities) between this nursing model and one of the medical models (e.g. that of Pendleton).
2   Draw a diagram to show how the *face* and the nursing models might be integrated.

Health-visiting model

Health visitors have quite a different focus.[14] Their goals are to promote health as follows:

* by maintaining and, over time, improving the dynamic equilibrium
* by heading off harmful stressors
* by enhancing clients' resistance resources/coping abilities
* by facilitating beneficial inputs in primary, secondary and tertiary prevention.

Differences from the nursing model are as follows.

1   The whole family is usually the client.
2   The focus is on needs, not on problems (related to health maintenance).
3   The focus is on stability, not on change.
4   There is serial activity over time (not disease episodes).

What do they really want?

> *Oh Master grant that I may never seek*
> *so much to be consoled as to console*
> *To be understood, as to understand*
> *To be loved as to love with all my soul*

(from the prayer of St Francis of Assisi)

Now there was a man who knew about the weakness of human nature.

It's all there in the consumer surveys – patients want to be heard, they want to be *understood*, and they want answers to their questions, proper explanations. Oh yes, and they want their health professionals to be competent as well.

That sounds perfectly reasonable, doesn't it? After all, they're paying, aren't they? Well, perhaps they should be paying a little more. Would we listen more if they were paying us directly? I'd really like to be able to say no to that question. How about you?

Why is it so vitally important to *understand* the other person's point of view? Well, actually, it is just as important to *communicate that you have understood.* This is perhaps the essential part of what Bendix called the therapeutic dialogue.[15] All of the insight in the world is a waste of time if the client/patient is unaware that you have it. You cannot cure a person with worn out joints, but you can show an interest in how it affects his or her life. Of course, there are options that might help in a practical way (ranging from appliances to joint replacements), but being recognised by another person is also important. Point of view and feelings are interwoven in a complex manner.

- As you get older, everything hurts.
- That which doesn't hurt doesn't work.
- Life is an incurable condition which all of us have.
- We all pass in the same general direction, though not by the same route.

Dr Strait, the senior district nurses and the midwife have no difficulty in relating to these thoughts, although when they had only recently qualified they might have seemed a little theoretical and far removed from their own experience. To Kerry-Ann, perhaps it makes little sense.

People out there make use of 'folk models' (why is this happening to me now, and what next?) to help to make sense of their symptoms and concerns, according to Helman.[16] They weigh up the consequences of action or inaction, often after discussion with family or friends. Beckman pointed out that the individual's decision to consult a professional is the result of a 'cascade of antecedents'.[17]

The patient's/client's agenda

This includes the following:

- problems/issues
- ideas/questions
- reasoning.

Look back at the box on the left-hand side of Figure 2.2.

Kerry-Ann has already told Dr Strait about her sore throat. There is another issue which might become a problem. Her period is three days late (she's normally as regular as clockwork), although she does feel as though she is about to 'come on'. Unfortunately, she had a sexual encounter during 'freshers' week'. She realises that she needs contraceptive advice, but is not sure whether to go to the Family Planning Clinic, or to ask this doctor (who looks about the same age as her father).

- She would like to ask how effective condoms are.
- She thinks that the pill would not be safe for her.
- She had not intended to embark on a new relationship, and she feels guilty because of her boyfriend at home.
- In the back of her mind is the thought that a sore throat could mean something more serious.
- She feels very alone in this new town, and is worried that she will not cope with the demands of the course.
- She is unsure how much of this she should tell Dr Strait, especially because he seems so busy and, in any case, might not approve.

Kerry-Ann used to think that a condom was pretty effective so long as the man used it properly, but now she's heard talk that disturbs her. Perhaps the sperm can get out around the edge? Perhaps a certain percentage of condoms are faulty and have microscopic holes?

She also believes that a past history of migraine means that one can't take the pill.

She knows that there could be many underlying causes of a sore throat, but is particularly worried about anything to do with the immune system. She has heard that AIDS can present as an increased susceptibility to infection.

I've tried to tease out the three layers of Kerry-Ann's agenda. This isn't always easy, as reasoning and ideas have a tendency to overlap. I'll try to clarify the difference as follows.

1   Ideas/questions – what do they think/want to ask?
2   Reasoning – why do they think that/want to ask that?

THINK BOX

How do you think poor Dr Strait would feel if he knew all this?

Would he be more comfortable with the 'nursing model', dealing with the whole person (of course with a longer appointment)?

As the practice nurse has to do a 'new-patient' check, could this kind of situation be addressed more effectively there?

Would another member of the primary healthcare team be more appropriate?

Well it could be that a major part of Dr Strait's problem, with a complex agenda such as Kerry-Ann's, is the feeling that doctors sometimes experience, that they (personally) have to solve every problem right now. You can probably see how shortage of time and a dysfunctional appointment system might contribute to such a feeling. However, to be able to use the full resources of the team, Dr Strait must understand their roles and be able to communicate with them. On a Monday morning it might seem easier not to discover the patient's agenda in all its glory. Is this a 'penicillin' sore throat or isn't it? Next please!

But wait – this is not such an extreme example, is it?

Kerry-Ann probably isn't pregnant and she probably hasn't got AIDS. Obviously if the period doesn't arrive soon, a test might be needed. If there seem to be grounds for concern, the local genito-urinary medicine (GUM) clinic will help. Otherwise the practice nurse can see her to give contraceptive advice/pill prescription.

She is a frightened lonely girl in a strange town, but her problems aren't unique. The practice team should be used to dealing with an influx of students every autumn.

Dr Strait has a daughter not much younger than this, and a father trembles for his daughter. You see, he does care. Besides, he's seen such problems before. Once upon a time he was a medical student himself. If only Kerry-Ann knew this.

Perhaps what she needs most out of the consultation is not penicillin, but to feel that the health professionals are on her side.

Another approach to the question 'what do they really want?', is provided by the simple framework devised by Stewart and colleagues.[18]

Reasons for consulting[18]

These include the following:

1   limit of anxiety
2   limit of tolerance
3   administrative
4   ticket of entry.

Kerry-Ann had perhaps reached her limit of anxiety about the possibility of pregnancy or AIDS. You could argue that this was her main reason for consulting, rather than the fact that she had reached her limit of tolerance of sore throat symptoms. However, people often display a mixture of these reasons for consulting. She had not come for the purpose of obtaining a sick-note or some other administrative reason, although Dr Strait was familiar with the scenario of students being asked to justify short-term absences from the college. The sore throat could well have been a 'ticket of entry'. Having produced this 'ticket', which was not her main concern, Kerry-Ann would perhaps have waited to see whether she was sufficiently sympathetically received for her to feel able to reveal the more personal part of her agenda.

So perhaps Dr Strait was right to assume that his 'minimalist' strategy would save him trouble. On the other hand, just what is being achieved in such a consultation? Also, how will some of his partners feel if all of the patients with time-consuming problems gravitate to them, whilst old Strait is left with all the 'quickies'?

A recipe for trouble at t'mill, I'd say.

A case of crossed wires

We have seen that Kerry-Ann and Dr Strait have very different agendas. Can any good come of this apparent mismatch?

The answer is not without the application of considerable communication skills (*see* Chapter 3).

The first problem is that neither of them is aware of the other's real agenda, which makes negotiation difficult. Unfortunately, this is a very common situation in medical consultations. Byrne and Long found that doctors frequently got the wrong end of the stick.[3] Tuckett and colleagues reported that doctors' actions often didn't seem relevant to patients' real concerns.[4] Cartwright and Anderson suggested that doctors ought to check that patients actually *want* a prescription before writing one.[19] Cromarty found that patients' explanatory models were often very different to those of their doctors.[20]

I keep focusing on doctors, I know. I hope it isn't too irritating for you other health professionals, but there is a reason for it.

To an extent, these problems of communication are generic. I'm sometimes reminded of scenes from my childhood, when I observed women (in headscarves) talking to each other on their doorsteps. It seemed to me that, whilst one of them was talking, the other would be taking a deep breath and waiting for the first to run out of the same. It was like two battleships firing salvoes past each other, neither of them really interested in the other's point of view.

Misunderstanding occurs in all forms of human interaction, even between nurses and patients, social workers and clients. It's just that the short *medical* consultation seems (on the basis of my observations) to maximise the potential for misunderstanding and conflict. I think it stems from two main causes:

1   pressure to make a diagnosis
2   shortage of time.

Formal application of 'clinical method' takes a long time. It also takes about two sides of A4 paper in the hospital notes. Doctors entering primary care for the first time tend to find it rather a shock, being expected to consult in five to 10 minutes and to record it in a few lines on the 'Lloyd George' card. Instead of coming to a considered diagnosis based on a long-winded systematic history, suddenly it is 'quick and dirty' methods that are needed.

But never fear – the hypothetico-deductive method will save the day! The *what?* Usually it's called 'guess and test'. It means making a provisional hypothesis relatively early on, and pursuing that line of questioning or investigation until it becomes necessary to guess again. It can be very effective, but it does depend on getting a high percentage of guesses right first time.

That is the problem. Guessing isn't really good enough. In order to make a decent *hypothesis*, as opposed to a guess, you need sufficient information.

1   Listen to the patient – they are telling you the diagnosis.
2   Listen to the other person – they are telling you something really important.

So what do doctors do?
According to Beckman and Frankel: [21]

* they interrupt after an average of 15 seconds
* they are desperate to make a diagnosis, and they know time is short
* they jump to premature conclusions
* they often guess wrong.

Hypotheses based on insufficient evidence are bad science. *Ask a silly question and you get a silly answer.*

EXERCISE

Look back at your own video or audio tape.

How soon do you interrupt your client/patient?

What effects does this have on subsequent proceedings?

Am I being unfair to doctors?

Do other health professionals have similar problems, or are they different?

What are the main pressures on other health professionals?

Dr Strait managed one 'Mmm' before he jumped in with his first question. He had to ask it twice, as if Kerry-Ann hadn't properly registered it first time. Then it seemed as though she couldn't be bothered to answer it, but he pursued the same line anyway (look back at the vignette).

He had apparently jumped to the conclusion that she wanted treatment for her viral sore throat. What evidence did he have for this hypothesis?

The scene was set for a possible conflict about antibiotics, and the main reason for the consultation might never have surfaced.

So far, then, premature conclusions – 1 and professional/client relationship – 0. However, it's only a half-time score.

Lessons not too late for the learning

Is anyone there? Sometimes it feels as if there isn't, but it's not too late – it doesn't *have* to be like this.

1   Try to understand the agenda of the other person. Remember:
   • issues
   • ideas/questions
   • reasoning.
2   Be aware of your own agenda and how far it might be conflicting.
3   Be prepared to negotiate outcomes.

Yes, it's the *face* again. But something's missing, isn't it?
How do you actually *do* all that?

By using communication skills, of course. And the good news is that you already have them. Roll on Chapter 3.

CHAPTER THREE

You can do it
ONE-TO-ONE
COMMUNICATION SKILLS

Donald says, 'I want bullet points:

- what to say
- how to position my body.'

Liam says, 'In communication, you've either got it or you haven't – and, let's *face* it, you haven't, Donald!'

   'It' – that is, the *skills* bit – is in the middle inverted triangle (the nose) of the *face* model.

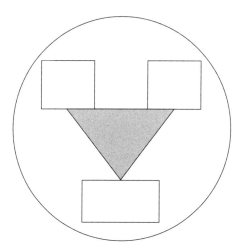

Figure 3.1

It's a question of attitude

I keep telling you that you already have the skills – and it's true (even for Donald). Okay, so I know that some of you would find it difficult to be television presenters. It takes all sorts. Some of us are noisy and some are quiet.

Just what have you been doing over the last few decades? Communicating with other people, among other things. What is more, you've all been trained as health professionals. It's your *job* to communicate with people – and you've been doing it, haven't you?

So there you are – it's just a question of degree.

However, there is always room for improvement – which is perhaps why you're here. You have the skills, rest assured, but what are you doing with them?

In fact, it's like walking or riding a bike. You could break those activities down into a great number of components, but normally you don't think about it. Your musculo-skeletal and nervous systems look after it automatically. Several years ago I tried (unsuccessfully) to learn how to ride a horse. I was doing fine, or so I thought, until the instructor told me not to sit as if I was riding a motor-bike when going round corners. I tried consciously to change my position and, of course, fell off at the next corner. Why pay good money to be laughed at? The skills for horse-riding never became automatic for me, but I haven't forgotten how to ride a bike.

You can learn communication skills, but by and large it's not like learning to drive a car from scratch. After all, you just have to tell yourself to walk backwards and you do it. It's the same with communication skills – just tell yourself to do what you know is necessary.

Be friendly.

That's not a bad instruction to start with, is it? Okay, I know Donald needs a bit more detail.

- Look at the other person.
- Try a little smile.

All right, Donald? Look, they're smiling back.

This may all seem rather obvious, but I once had to teach a registrar to do this in consultations. Even then, he already knew how to smile and make eye contact. It was more a question of my giving permission for him to use skills he already had.

I am reminded of a book I once read called *Improving your Football*, by Jimmy Hill, in which there are detailed descriptions of relevant skills, including tackling. Having dealt with the details, Hill comes up with a marvellous statement: '*If you want the ball badly enough, your body will find a way to get it for you!*'

I'm not sure how this would fit in with the new FIFA rules, but you get the point, don't you? It's all a question of *attitude*. Do you really *want* to know why the patient or client has come to see you? Wanting to do something is more than half the battle.

Your body already knows what to do. It only needs broad instructions from the higher reaches of your mind. Be confident. Use yourself – a unique individual with your own solutions which have evolved during your development.

Be friendly.

Find out why they're here.

If you're not confident of your own ability, try role-playing someone else. Health professionals do it all the time. I used to find I was better at football when I pretended to be someone famous (I won't tell you who, in case you laugh).

Act friendly

It's all a question of attitude.

This approach of letting a solution emerge from your inner self is quite similar to that advocated by Roger Neighbour,[1,2] in his two books on teaching and consulting, and in contrast to the behavioural (micro-teaching) approach of David Pendleton.[3] Both approaches work. You *can* learn communication skills and you *can* release those you already have.

How would you like your health professional to behave?

Let's try to be a little client/patient-centred.

THINK BOX

When did you last see your doctor, nurse or health visitor (or any other member of the primary healthcare team)?

What did you like about their approach?

What didn't you like about their approach?

What exactly do you want from your health visitor, nurse, doctor, etc.?

So how did you feel about being on the other side of the fence for once?

From my point of view, the doctor is fine, but I do find the receptionists a bit of a problem. Or is it the other way round? I can only answer for myself.

I want my doctor to provide a welcoming atmosphere which enables me to tell him or her, in my own words, what is on my mind. I also want him or her to give me advice or to take appropriate measures to address those issues. That's about it. How does that compare with your answers?

Oh yes! I'd almost forgotten. There is something else on my wish list. I'm not sure how to say this, but here goes.

I want to be respected.

There! My little hang-up is out in the open. I'm still in the role of a patient, you understand. Actually, I think that it's a basic human right for all people to be respected. And I also think that's almost the other half of the battle in communication.

So what is respect?

It's about recognising and valuing the other person's individuality, autonomy and ideas, and being tolerant of their beliefs and attitudes.

Doesn't this remind you of the nursing model of Roper and colleagues[4] in Chapter 2?

EXERCISE

Replay your video or audio tape of encounters with your patients/clients.

Mark yourself on the client-centred parameters you have just produced.

How did you measure up?

Did you help them to share their agenda with you?

Did you respect them?

What a wonderful health professional you are.

The trouble is that my tape is all from Monday morning!

Active perception both ways

Are you really really convinced yet about the absolute, paramount, overriding importance of understanding the client's or patient's point of view in the process of communication?

Yeah, yeah!

Okay. Look, I'm sorry to be such a pain, but I have a problem in this way of communicating with you. You see I'm getting no feedback – it's so frustrating. If you were here in front of me, you could tell me to shut up because you know what I'm telling you already. Or you could shift uncomfortably in your seat so that, if I weren't so thick-skinned, I would know that I'm boring you.

The thing, then, is to understand the agenda of the other person – to know where they are coming from – before you try to explain what they don't want to hear, or solve problems that interest only you.

You've got to listen *actively* as if your life depends on it. And not only to listen, but to look, and perhaps even smell or feel. At one time, doctors used to taste patients' urine (perhaps the good old days weren't so brilliant after all).

You must use all of your faculties to make sure that you understand.

Why? Because the interview or consultation is going nowhere unless you do.

Imagine yourself as a radar scanner, with the dish representing all of the apparatus you have at your disposal (your five senses – and perhaps even a sixth sense). You're sitting quietly and alert. A lot of information is coming into that dish, but it's not dropping into an empty container. Your brain has to learn how to make sense of all the signals it receives, and yours has been doing that, and perfecting its technique, over many years. Signals are not just received but they are also *interpreted* in the light of your own individual experience. Judgement is never completely suspended, is it?

Radar scanner model

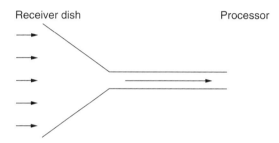

Figure 3.2

What I am talking about is a state of relative openness at the beginning of the interview. It may well be necessary to move on to a more problem-solving phase later, and this is represented by the tube or processor part of the model. There is some similarity to the hypothetico-deductive (or 'guess and test') model of Chapter 2. However, there are two important points to remember.

- The radar dish has to be really wide and supersensitive.
- If you find yourself in the processor part of the apparatus, don't completely shut off power from the dish. Be prepared to abandon or revise your hypothesis if fresh signals are at variance with it.

In two-way communication between A and B there is a cycle of signal sending and receiving, with the brains of each protagonist working overtime to interpret what is happening, so that output is continually modified in relation to what is received.

Figure 3.3

Whilst you are working out what messages will be appropriate for your patient or client, they are also paying attention to your signals, to try to establish what is appropriate to tell you. Remember how much Kerry-Ann didn't say to Dr Strait in Chapter 2.

So perception is active in two ways:

- being 'switched on' to receive information
- it cannot be passive, because interpretation occurs all the time (try as you might).

I hope Donald appreciates all of these bullet points.

Let's now take a look at the signals in a little more detail.

What messages am I giving out?

Do you play a good hand of poker? Donald does. However, Liam cannot stop being 'touchy-feely'. You can always read his face.

Perhaps the most obvious part of a message is its content – that is, the *verbal communication*. Words have the meaning that we assign to them. People from the south of England might not realise that, when I describe something as 'all right', I am using a superlative. You have to earn praise in the East Midlands.

'What do you think of my new dress, dear?'

(Looking up from the football supplement)'It's all right.'

Slap! (So volatile, these Southerners.)

You don't have to travel very far to find examples of difficulties in communication. My patients in Loughborough tell me that they have problems understanding people from Shepshed (about five miles away), although I think they could be exaggerating (either that, or Shepshed is now full of commuters from Leicester).

One difficulty is that different people mean different things by the same words. For example, if a Scotsman complains of a 'sore' toe, you'd better suspect gangrene. In the East Midlands, the word 'sore' refers to a much more low-key sensation, that is hardly worthy of the term 'pain'.

Another problem is that, with different dialects, familiar words may sound unintelligible to an outsider, or the words themselves may be peculiar to that district. 'Ganging (or 'gannin') hame' means 'going home' in the North East. 'Kelter' means 'rubbish' (residue in the lime kilns of the Peak District of Derbyshire).

Bullet points for Donald:

*   language is understood in different ways
*   language is not understood at all.

'Ah've gorra sore throat an worravyoh' (to quote a man who once came to see me in Loughborough).

For those who want a literal translation, the last 'word' is 'what have you'. Does that get us any further forward? What do you expect to get with sore throats? A headache? A temperature? Aching all over? Does 'worravyoh' mean I've got the full house of symptoms, therefore please hand over the antibiotics? Or is it perhaps being used as punctuation, or almost as an expletive?

'Nice day an worravyoh.'

(Looking in the direction of Shepshed): 'Yeah, but it looks like rain an worravyoh.'

We have enough problems with the English language ourselves. Foreigners have my sympathy. Interpreters are of course extremely helpful, but you don't know exactly what they are saying to the other party (and therefore how much it might have changed in the translation), and vice versa.

EXERCISE

Play your audio or video tape again.

Can you find any examples of situations where there appears to be misunderstanding connected with the meaning of language?

Were you aware of it at the time? Be honest.

How did you deal with those misunderstandings?

If you can't find any examples of overt misunderstandings of that kind, look for language which has the potential to be misunderstood.

So much for the content of the message.

However, messages also come in a wrapper. This is the *non-verbal communication*. In Donald's case, it's a bit sparse, but it's still there if you know what to look for. This could be vital if you're playing for money. As for Liam, well, he may appear to wear his heart on his sleeve, but what you see is not necessarily what you get. However, we have ways of finding him out.

What is in the 'wrapping'?

- The sound of the voice (tone, pitch, volume, modulation, etc.).
- Non-verbal utterances (mmm, uhuh, etc.).
- Gestures.
- Eye contact.
- Facial expression.
- Involuntary movements (e.g. 'fidgeting').
- Touch.
- Smell (sometimes?).
- Style (dress, etc.).

The potential for ambiguity now becomes even greater.

If I raise my voice, does that mean I'm angry? Or is it when I go quiet that you have to be careful? You'd have to know me.

Dr Strait notices that Kerry-Ann's voice goes up in pitch at the end of each sentence. Does this mean that she's anxious, or has she simply been watching too many Australian 'soaps'?

Does Dr Strait's 'mmm' at the beginning of the consultation mean that he's listening or just impatient?

My habit of wagging my index and little fingers at the same time may indicate that I'm considering some kind of dilemma, but in some parts of Europe the same gesture might be taken as a gross insult (meaning that someone else is sleeping with your wife). You really cannot be too careful in a cosmopolitan place like Loughborough.

Some people barely make any eye contact at all, whilst others engage in a constant stare, as though it's some kind of contest. Either extreme can be difficult to deal with. More often, eye contact occurs at junctions in a conversation, to check whether the other person is still listening, or to confirm to the speaker that you are still following them.

As for facial expression, can you interpret the smile of the Mona Lisa or the expression of the Sphinx? I'll tell you for free that, when I knit my brows, it means I'm really paying attention to what you're saying, not that I disapprove of the content.

Are you a 'toucher'? I'm not, so keep off! I need plenty of personal space, thank you. Other people get used to how you are – perhaps it's a change that is significant? If I suddenly started to touch people in order to illustrate points during a conversation, I think everyone would be extremely worried.

Do you use your handshake as a game of dominance (for men only)? Okay, so what *am* I supposed to infer from the pressure of your hand, or the lack of it?

Have you ever smelt fear? Or was it just a hot day?

What am I trying to say to you by not wearing a tie?

What are you trying to say to me by dressing up to the nines? Or are you just on the way to somewhere else?

As we now know from the script, Kerry-Ann's wringing of her hands whilst she talks about her sore throat probably indicates a degree of distress associated with an underlying problem.

Hands and feet tell you when something does not fit. Facial expression is much more likely to be under conscious control.

There's the key to beating both Liam and Donald at poker.

EXERCISE

Play your video or audio tape again.

What messages were you sending by your non-verbal behaviour?

Were those messages consistent with the verbal content, or was there some degree of conflict?

What messages were you receiving from the client or patient?

Did you pay attention to those messages, or did you ignore or fail to register some of them?

How easy was it for you to interpret the non-verbal behaviour of your client or patient?

Can you find examples of your non-verbal behaviour *mirroring* that of your client or patient?

What do you think mirroring means in the context of your own consultations?

What does it mean when behaviour is in contrast (for example, one person leaning forward and the other leaning back)?

Communicating is risk-taking

All the time we're giving out both verbal and non-verbal signals, the potential for ambiguity and misunderstanding is enormous.

The words I use and the non-verbal behaviour I display are connected with my family, my wider social group with its history and geography, and my subsequent experiences. You could attempt to categorise my behaviour in terms of a 'tribal' group with certain socio-economic characteristics, but to an extent that would be to deny my individuality. You see *I'm not like the rest.* I read books, listen to the radio, watch television, and I've even been to the Isle of Wight. So you see, the outside world has begun to dilute my group membership. Don't let my accent mislead you either, because I'm such a good mimic.

You can't be sure of the meaning of anything I say or do. I can't be sure of anything about you either. Isn't it exciting?

Communication is so *risky!* Much safer to stay in your dark cave and meet no one.

In communication, meaning must be constantly negotiated.

It's like an amoeba putting out a pseudopodium (two amoebae, in fact). My first move is very tentative, as I don't like having my pseudopodia trodden on. No, it doesn't feel right. Withdraw and try another tack. That other guy looks so amorphous. Just what is his angle?

Kerry-Ann: 'My throat is really really sore.'
Dr Strait thinks of the following possibilities:

- perhaps she wants penicillin
- perhaps she's very worried about the sore throat
- perhaps she wants a note for college
- perhaps she's saying *please listen*
- perhaps she's been watching too many Australian soaps
- perhaps she's Scottish and her tonsils are about to turn black.

Perhaps you can generate some other possibilities?

Dr Strait: 'Are you really worried about your sore throat?'
Kerry-Ann: 'Course I'm not worried – can't you give me something for it?'

Dr Strait is feeling rather silly. One slightly bruised pseudopodium is quietly withdrawn. Why don't I just write a prescription next time, instead of all this 'touchy-feely' stuff?

Nurses might have a different approach, being less fixated on solving problems (is this fair comment?).

Kerry-Ann: 'My throat is really really sore.'
Sister O'Mercy: 'That must be terrible for you.'

Should Dr Strait try that type of approach? In fact, if you remember, what he originally said was 'Mmm'.

Why didn't that work?

Working out a suitable response to another person is very much an intuitive process. We do the best we can with the information that we have available. Often we seem to get it wrong. Well, I do (if we're going to get into ownership of statements).

EXERCISE

Try to find examples on your tape of situations where you put out feelers and then had to withdraw them.

Having been rebuffed, do you think you were definitely wrong in your initial assumptions?

If you were wrong, was that because you were not attending carefully enough to the other person's non-verbal signals?

In some cases, is it possible that you were right all along, despite the client's or patient's reaction to the contrary?

Why do you think this was so?

What made the other person deny it?

How did you recover from the experience of being rebuffed (if you did)?

It is not only the meaning which must be negotiated.

In communication the situation and roles must also be negotiated.

Some people want to make all of the decisions themselves, and use their health professionals as a source of some of the information to support those decisions. At the other extreme, the health professional is expected to be directive, and the patient or client follows their instructions without question. Between these two extremes there lie varying degrees of shared decision-making. Perhaps this reminds you of the 'parent–adult– child' model of Eric Berne,[5] which was described in Chapter 2.

Moveover, roles and situations are not fixed for each person or combination of people. For example, Erikson tells us that, in times of illness or stress, it is quite common for people to regress back to the 'child' state.[6]

When I had chest pain (among other symptoms), I didn't want to discuss the differential diagnosis and probabilities with my doctor. I just wanted him to tell me it was all right. As soon as he told me that it was a virus, the pain began to fade into the background. Have you been in a similar situation, where you wanted to be looked after by a parent figure, and to hand over the responsibility to them?

Part of finding out about the other person's agenda is to work out what sort of role they wish to play in the transaction with you. For example, elderly people are often less keen on the 'sharing approach', and may lose confidence if the professional appears to be asking them what to do. However, not everyone is the same, and it is always risky to make assumptions. In any case, it may be misleading because the previous generation may be acting on the basis of experience with health professionals of the 'old school'.

There is no point in telling Sister Brasstoff what you think. It is much safer to go along with the old battleaxe.

EXERCISE

Can you find examples on your tape of situations or roles that were being negotiated?

How did you do it? (For example: 'Let me get this straight – are you asking me to tell you what to do?')

Did you try to avoid responsibility sometimes when you should really have taken it on?

Did the roles remain constant throughout the same interviews?

Do you have a preferred role?

Why?

Put out a pseudopodium and test the water.
Be prepared to withdraw it if the situation demands this.
Don't you just love the frisson you get with risk-taking?
It is now time to be more specific.

Parts of the interview

Donald has his notebook poised. Liam is about to nod off.

In a way it is easy to demonstrate how an interview divides up into natural sections – for example, a beginning, a middle and an end. Byrne and Long's model[7] *(see* Chapter 2) seems to be based on events that take place in a certain order. However, you have probably noticed from your own video or audio tapes that it is often difficult to label a sequence of events because there tends to be a great deal of to-ing and fro-ing. Pendleton found the same thing with his 'consultation maps' of tasks against time.[3]

THINK BOX

Why should there be so much jumping about from one task to another?

If you were more skilled at communicating, would you be better able to maintain a tidy and logical sequence?

Donald thinks so. You can imagine Liam's expression.

If it is difficult to keep to a sequence of events; a list of tasks to be achieved (such as that of Pendleton and colleagues; *see* Chapter 2) might be more useful. I'm just about to invent another model. No, you don't have to learn it! This is only to try to help us go through the parts of an interview, so that we can think about the specific skills needed on the way. I don't want anything too complicated.

Not quite the *face* model

This consists of the following:

*   gathering information (rapport, facilitation, clarification)
*   processing (self-awareness, negotiation, management)
*   concluding (presentation, forward planning).

There! That didn't hurt much, did it?

I'll explain the subdivisions of these bullet points as we go along.

Gathering information

Exploring the other person's agenda, clarifying it and playing it back can be a form of treatment if, by doing this, the other becomes more self-aware and able to generate their own solutions to problems. This is the basis of *non-directive counselling.*

The client gains insight (which is sometimes painful) and solutions through verbalisation of problems.

The role of the counsellor is to give the client *undivided uncritical attention.* The counsellor does *not* tell the client what to do, nor does he or she advise, reassure, explain or encourage.

THINK BOX

Health professionals often tell clients what to do, etc.

Health professionals do not always give clients undivided uncritical attention.

Do you agree?

Or is this only true of some health professionals (e.g. doctors)?

Do you think that health professionals have anything to learn from non-directive counsellors?

What will you learn and how will you apply it?

Rapport

When would you say that you have rapport with your health visitor or doctor? Is your answer something like 'when it feels like they're on your wavelength'? How do you know when they are?

Is it because they're paying attention to your concerns and helping you to work out the best ways of dealing with them? You've probably had a smile and some eye contact. They're probably not fiddling with their notes or the computer, or making distracting body movements. You feel *respected*. Or perhaps you already know them well, and you can overlook their 'below par' performance today because of your previous favourable experience of them.

Well, I think that it's all in the skills below. Get them right and you've got rapport.

EXERCISE

Play your video or audio tape again.

Are there any other ingredients of rapport in your own performance as a health professional?

Write them in this space.

Facilitation

Are you ready, Donald?

Facilitation is helping the other person to produce their story. Here are the skills:

- open questions
- attending behaviour
- minimal encouragers
- lowering barriers.

Open questions allow a wide range of responses. Examples would include 'Tell me about it' or 'Why do you think that?'. The opposite would allow only a narrow range of responses – in the extreme case either 'Yes' or 'No'. Examples of closed questions would include 'How long have you had this?' or 'Do you feel tired with it?'. Open questions help the client or patient to tell their story in their own way, without interference by the health professional.

Attending behaviour shows the other person that you're still there in mind as well as in body – and that you're still awake to their concerns. Appropriate *eye contact* and *bodily attitude* are helpful. Some individuals will be put off by your leaning forward and staring, although the opposite behaviour could be interpreted as lack of interest. Be sensitive to individual and cultural variations. Learn to negotiate with your body language (she's shrinking back – perhaps I'm a bit too near for her?). *Verbal following* also demonstrates attention – for example,'You say your throat's really sore'. Sometimes the repetition of the last word or phrase is very effective – for example,'...been up all night with it'.

However, if in doubt, leave a gap *(use silence)* or try some *minimal encouragers*. The latter signal that it's all right for the other person to carry on talking, but they are not so obtrusive as to obstruct the flow of the story. Examples of *verbal* encouragers include 'Go on', 'mmm' or 'uhuh'. Non-verbal encouragers would include head nodding or spreading the hands. Again, you have to be alert to individual or cultural differences when interpreting these signs. In particular, watch the other person's body language – is there something which does not seem to be consistent with what you're hearing?

Lowering barriers is sometimes necessary to enable the patient or client to tell their story. The type of message you may need to get across is 'It's all right to tell me' or 'I promise I won't laugh' or 'Lots of people have this problem'. You can tell when you need this skill because the other person may hesitate, stop or exhibit signs of anxiety (watch the hands in particular). You should also monitor your own body language and make sure that it isn't too threatening for that individual.

EXERCISE

Review your audio or video tape for facilitation skills.

Make a list of your deficiencies by reference to the skills listed above.

What are your main priorities?

Practise the skills you need by role-playing with a colleague or (ideally) a simulated patient or client.

Remember: the most important part of the skill is wanting to do it.

Now make use of these newly polished skills in your next encounter with clients or patients.

Make another recording of your improved self.

What are your priorities now?

Kerry-Ann: 'Doctor, my throat is really really sore....'
Dr Strait: 'Mmm...' (He leans slightly forward, and notices that she's playing with her hands.)
Kerry-Ann: 'And I feel really really hot.' (She hesitates.)
Dr Strait (notices the hesitation, leans slightly back and smiles encouragingly): 'Go on'
Kerry-Ann: 'And there's something else, too...'
Dr Strait (nods his head, opens his hands and adopts a more relaxed position).

What a lovely doctor. You'd tell him anything, wouldn't you?
Notice all the skills he's using, although it seems as if he's barely doing anything.
That appeals to Liam.

Clarification

Clarification is making sure that you have understood the story.

It also shows the other person that you are trying to understand and, finally, that you have understood what they are trying to communicate to you.

Because it tends to be more intrusive than facilitation, you should make sure that the other person has had sufficient opportunity to tell their story before you jump in with too many of these techniques (try listening to a news reporter interviewing a politician).

The following skills are needed (although there are no hard and fast rules – for example, you might find yourself using open questions as well as closed ones):

• closed questions
• paraphrasing
• reflecting feelings
• concreteness
• summarising.

We have already seen examples of *closed questions* in the previous section. They are useful for checking on information which you have absorbed imperfectly, or which seems to be incomplete. For example, 'Did you say both ears were hurting?' or 'Did this pain go away when you were having all that extra work to take home?'. The second question could also be testing a hypothesis.

Paraphrasing is a useful way of checking your understanding of part of the message. You feed back in your own words what you think you've just heard. For example, 'Are you saying that your mother-in-law gives you a migraine?' In this way you invite the other person to correct your interpretation. Of course it is risky, but so is all communication (so go back under your stone, Donald!). I never get migraine, so it's quite a safe example for me to use.

Reflecting feelings is perhaps even more risky. 'I have the impression that you're a teensy-weensy bit angry' might be good for triggering a volcanic eruption. Still, sometimes you need to know what the mismatch between the other person's apparent message and their body language means. Sometimes it is obvious what is happening. For example, if your client or patient is drying their eyes with a tissue, it probably helps to acknowledge the situation and use techniques to lower the barriers. The subject of feelings will be covered in more detail in Chapter 4, but the key to it lies in non-verbal behaviour.

Concreteness involves getting down to the nitty-gritty. People can be unconsciously or deliberately vague, especially when they are describing something they find difficult or distressing. Perhaps they hope that you can read accurately between the lines, so that they can avoid verbalising something which is painful to them. Here is an example of being concrete: 'I wasn't sure if you were saying that you had been sexually abused.' Also pretty risky, don't you think? Often, however, with a problem like that, if you don't ask a direct question you will never find out even if the other person wants you to.

Summarising is pretty self-explanatory, I should think. I'm sure you all know how to do it. It's just a question of telling yourself to – in the right place. When you think that you've got the gist of the story, or at least that you've come to the end of a significant part of it, play it back to the other person and ask them if you've got it right. This will probably involve the skill of paraphrasing, which we've already discussed. However, you must learn to be brief, whilst at the same time retaining all of the important points, otherwise the other person's attention may start to wander.

'Just let me recap. You'd like to know how you can stop the baby crying at night, because your husband works shifts and he says it's your fault for not breast-feeding. Is that right?'

Is that punchy or what (as a health-visitor friend of mine might have said)?

Again it's a bit risky, but, if you're barking up the wrong tree, it's best to find out before your interview time runs out.

EXERCISE

Review your audio or video tape for clarification skills.

Make a list of your deficiencies by reference to the skills listed above.

What are your main priorities?

Practise the skills you need by role-playing with a colleague or (ideally) a simulated patient or client.

Remember: the most important part of the skill is wanting to do it.

Now make use of these newly polished skills in your next encounter with clients or patients.

Make another recording of your improved self.

What are your priorities now?

Kerry-Ann: 'Actually, my period's three days late and..., I know this might sound silly...'

Dr Strait: 'No, not at all.'

Kerry-Ann: 'But I'm normally regular as clockwork. Anyway, I did sleep with someone in freshers' week, although he did wear something... but I don't know much about condoms, how effective they are, and...'

Dr Strait: 'Mmm..'

Kerry-Ann: 'I'm so ashamed because of my boyfriend at home. It's because I'm lonely here... and now I'm really really worried too' (she looks down suddenly). 'Do you think it could be worry causing it, doctor?'

Dr Strait: 'That's quite possible' (he leans over and touches her shoulder). 'You poor thing; you're in quite a state, aren't you? There's a box of tissues if you need them. No, don't worry about crying – it's quite all right' (he pauses). 'You've got quite a plateful of troubles, haven't you? You're worried about being pregnant, feeling guilty about letting your boyfriend down, you're isolated, without any friends in a strange town, and now you've got this awful virus which is making you feel even worse. Is that about right, or is there more?'

Kerry-Ann: (shakes her head).

Dr Strait: 'What about sexually transmitted disease? Is that a worry for you, too?'

Kerry-Ann: (nods her head slowly).

Dr Strait: 'All right. Well, let's look at each of these worries in turn. Tell me, did he wear a condom before he went inside you?'

THINK BOX

What skills was Dr Strait using in this part of the interview?

How would you have handled the situation?

The patient's/client's agenda

In the *face* model, this is the top left-hand box.

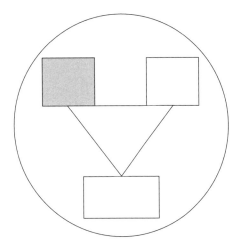

Figure 3.4

In the sequence we have been following, the corresponding skills are those of information-gathering – that is, *rapport, facilitation and clarification.*

Remember, though, that I had proposed the following three layers of the other's agenda:

- problems/issues
- ideas/questions
- reasoning.

People often find it difficult to expose all of these layers, perhaps because they still find health professionals intimidating, or maybe because the underlying layers are difficult for them to admit even to themselves.

The fear of AIDS is one example where people might not want to face reality, and where there is often a degree of ignorance, leading to reluctance to be exposed to potential ridicule by the health professional.

Letting people know in advance that their ideas will be valued and that they will be respected is a powerful way of lowering barriers to eliciting the full agenda.

Kerry-Ann: '...My period's three days late and...I know this might sound silly.'

Dr Strait: 'Don't worry about that. It *helps* me to know what you think.'

Asking a direct question, as Dr Strait did about sexually transmitted disease, can be useful if the hunch is right, but it could also provoke denial if the situation is too confrontational. Sometimes it works better to lower the barriers by making it seem more like a problem which many other people also have. This is known as the technique of *running up a flag to see if anyone salutes* or, in Roger Neighbour's book, the *my friend, John, technique.*[1]

Dr Strait: 'Lots of people might be worried about AIDS in this situation.'

Kerry-Ann: 'Oh.'

Dr Strait (pauses): 'I knew a young student, just like yourself, who spent a long time worrying about it, even though the actual risk was low.'

Kerry-Ann: 'Well, now you come to mention it...'

Dr Strait: 'Tell me why you think there might be a problem.'

Kerry-Ann: 'You're probably going to tell me I'm stupid, but it's this sore throat. I've heard that AIDS suppresses your immune system, and getting frequent infections could be the first sign of it.'

Dr Strait: 'I'm glad you've told me this. I'll try and sort out the worries, but first I'll need to ask some more questions and perhaps examine you, before we decide whether any tests are needed. Is that OK, or are there any other things you want to tell me?'

Do remember however, that *the most important part of the skill is really wanting to find out.*

Processing

When you have taken in the information from the other party, it has to be *processed* by your mental apparatus. This involves integration of your own agenda as a health professional, which requires *self-awareness*, and *negotiation* with the client or patient in order to determine priorities for the *management* of mutually important issues.

Liam thinks that sounds a bit technical. Donald doesn't know what it means either, but he thinks it sounds good (sad man).

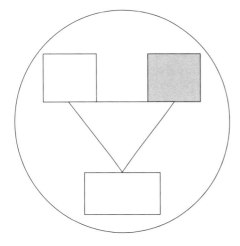

Figure 3.5

Self-awareness

The professional must be aware of the different components of his or her agenda. These include the following:

- discovering the other's agenda (hopefully we've done that in the previous section)
- considering (and completing) the database (continuing and dormant issues, and risk factors)
- problem-solving
- private agenda (institution, outside world, personal).

You have already met this framework in the guise of the doctor's agenda in Chapter 2 (top right-hand box in the *face* model). Being self-aware gives you an opportunity to prevent those parts of your agenda which are not in the interests of your patient or client from intruding. Neighbour calls this *housekeeping*.[1]

Dr Strait may have got out of bed on the wrong side this morning (he's not the only one – remember it is Monday), but poor Kerry-Ann shouldn't have to suffer for that. It's time to be a true professional. Never mind the fact that you've had no sleep and you're surrounded by a sea of disaster at home and away. Look up and take an interest! Stop fiddling with that computer – you should have looked at it before. Concentrate on what's important *right now*. Go through the above framework in your head (do the paperwork afterwards or it will interfere with the process).

Negotiation

- What does the client *want* from you? (Client's agenda).
- What does the client *need* from you? (Professional's agenda).

These are the essential elements for negotiation.

I'm talking, of course, about negotiation between health professionals and their clients, not about what happens between two neighbours like Liam and Donald, let alone between a salesperson and a customer (*see* Chapter 1).

THINK BOX

What do you think is the difference?

Does it depend on the extent to which the health professional can turn his or her wants into the needs of the client?

Isn't that what being a professional means?

Is the answer always so clear-cut?

Kerry-Ann wants help with her problems.

Dr Strait wants to complete the database on her (which is also in her interest, you could argue).

He is also under pressure to go for a quick solution, avoiding too many follow-ups (which is probably not in her interest).

Finally, he is suffering from 'burnout' (which is definitely not in her interest).

Nevertheless, patients or clients do not expect their health professionals to exploit them for their own ends, as sometimes happens in transactions with other people out there in the big cruel world. Otherwise it's a case for the General Medical Council and the Sunday papers.

A large part of 'negotiation' in the healthcare interview seems to involve checking back with the client that the next thing is acceptable. The proposed next step may be an interpretation of the client's wishes, or it may be something that the professional considers to be an appropriate response.

'You want me to listen to your chest. Is that all right?'

'It seems like you'd prefer me to tell you what I think is the best option, or would you rather have the information so you can decide?'

'I need to have a detailed description of your diet over the last week. Okay?'

Dr Strait: 'I'm going to need to do an internal examination. All right?'

Kerry-Ann (shifting uncomfortably in her chair): 'Well...'

Dr Strait (picking up the non-verbal signals, bless him): 'If you'd rather see a lady doctor for that, I can arrange another appointment for you. The reason you need this examination is so that some samples can be sent off to the laboratory.'
Kerry-Ann: 'Perhaps it would be as well to get it over with now.'
Dr Strait: 'Are you sure about that? Would you like me to arrange for a chaperone to be present?'
Kerry-Ann: 'No, no. I'd just feel worse. It's all right, really.'

I know some of you smart guys are already picking holes in poor old Strait's clinical management. Doctors are really awful like that. I can see your supercilious smiles, but just remember this is only a story.

Did you notice what happened in transactional terms, however?

Crafty old Strait got her to agree to something that she had initially rejected. He persuaded her that the thing she didn't want at first was now something she did want.

Remember the salesman in Chapter 1. He persuaded Fred that he wanted a more expensive car. He used Fred's feelings of inferiority.

Strait used Kerry-Ann's fears about venereal disease. The only difference is that Strait's intentions are benign – we hope.

It is possible for health professionals, like salesmen, to manipulate outcomes by 'hooking' into the client's agenda so that they begin to want what their doctor or nurse or social worker thinks they need. How far this is ethical is a matter for argument in individual cases. It is very easy to overstep the mark.

'You say you value your independence? Well, you'll never have any unless you leave that house.'

Sometimes negotiation is a game of give and take, where there are mutual concessions. I've given you an antibiotic, now you come to my health promotion clinic. You stop smoking and then I'll do your operation. Very dodgy, that one.

These types of games do take place but, on the whole, it is better to avoid manipulation and subterfuge in healthcare transactions. It might work, and it might be in the client's interest, but they'll probably find out what you did in the end.

Respect the other person – it's the best way to create trust.

- As far as possible, be open about your agenda, and encourage your patient or client to be the same.
- Try to summarise your perception of the two points of view and work out how they can best work together in the client's interest.
- Generate options and be prepared to discuss the advantages and disadvantages of each.
- Ensure that the client is able to give informed consent to the plan of management.

Dr Strait: ' You could have an antibiotic for your throat, but I'm not sure that it's the best thing to do, for a number of reasons. Perhaps the most important one is that the experts are now saying that it makes no difference with viruses. On the other hand, if you wait a little longer it might be difficult to get another appointment this week. If things are getting a lot worse, you have my permission to tell the receptionist that it's urgent and you'll be fitted in at the end of morning surgery.'

Kerry-Ann: 'I'm not so worried about the throat now you've explained it might be part of the flu. I'd just like my mind put at rest about pregnancy and whether I might have caught something nasty.'

Dr Strait: 'Well, now we have to decide how long to wait before you might need a pregnancy test, if your period doesn't come. Also we have to decide whether that contact you had was at all risky and, if so, whether you might be better off going to the special clinic where they have all the right equipment for the tests.'

Marks out of ten for Strait? Could do better?

It's not easy to negotiate adequately in a short consultation. Is the answer to train (and pay for) more health professionals? Or is it to charge fees to discourage time-wasters (or just the underprivileged)?

If you can square the circle, you can be the next Prime Minister.

Management

In clinical medicine, 'management' is a process which depends on history and examination – in other words, on the diagnosis. For example, Kerry-Ann's sore throat could be managed by prescribing penicillin (diagnosis of tonsillitis), or just by explanation and reassurance (diagnosis of viral infection). Either option would need a 'safety net' or explicit arrangements for follow-up.

However, as I argued in Chapter 2, there is more to life in primary care than diagnoses, at least in the clinical sense. Also, I prefer to view 'management' in a more global sense.

Management involves dealing with the agendas.

- You've discovered why the patient or client is there and what they want.
- You've thought about what you want to achieve on behalf of this individual.
- Management is what you do with the information.

Negotiating skills are needed to ensure that your broad aims, specific priorities and methods of achieving them are agreed with the patient or client. This view of management is independent of diagnosis, and may include further history-taking (what Byrne and Long called a 'verbal examination')[7] or physical examination. For example, a patient who has come for reassurance that they haven't got pneumonia could be managed by listening to their chest. In other cases, the management may consist purely of listening, on the basis that 'a trouble shared is a trouble halved'. Some people who frequently attend may have no one else but a health professional available to perform this function. The problems are often insoluble, and indeed it may be counter-productive to try to solve them.

EXERCISE

Review your tape again and think about your own agendas (including personal or extraneous ones) for each encounter.

How far were you aware of them at the time? (Be honest about this.)

Were your negotiations 'above board', or were you sometimes manipulative? Or did you negotiate at all?!

If you were manipulative, can you justify it?

Are you sure?

Were your methods of management appropriate in the circumstances?

Would your clients or patients agree?

How far does your management style tend towards the clinical model?

Set some priorities for yourself in the field of 'processing'.

Practise new techniques with colleagues or simulators.

Record another clinical session.

How far have you achieved your priorities?

Set some new priorities and repeat the process.

Concluding

Concluding takes place when you wrap it all up at the end, and send the patient or client on their way. Or perhaps they send you on your way?

You need *presentation skills* to remind the client how far they've come, and *forward-planning skills* to help to ensure a safe journey from here.

You'll go far in politics, my friend.

Donald is ready with his flip chart. Liam intends to improvise. 'You mean "waffle"', says Donald.

Presentation

Consider the following points:

- revisit the plan you agreed
- has it been carried out?
- does the result satisfy the client's agenda?
- is there unfinished business?

You need to make a summary of what has happened so far. If you cover the above points, it will be relevant to your client and they will probably listen. If they keep interrupting, it might be because you've missed part of their agenda along the way (that'll teach you). You now have a choice of starting the interview again or postponing the issue for another appointment. That rather depends on the problem, doesn't it? How urgent is urgent?

In your presentation, remember the following points:

- salient points (or you'll bore them)
- no jargon (or you'll lose them)
- check their understanding
- consider the use of written material.

> Dr Strait: 'Having examined you, I'm sure that this is a virus, so you don't need antibiotics. I hope I've reassured you that you're at low risk from AIDS, and having a virus so soon after the encounter isn't an early sign of it. From what you've told me, it also seems unlikely that you would be pregnant. However, we've agreed that we need to make sure about both of these worries. I think you may benefit from a general and lifestyle check-up'.
> Kerry-Ann: 'Yes, but I'm still worried.'
> Dr Strait (briskly): 'That's understandable. Now let's plan where we go from here.'

How did Strait score on the above points?
What would you have done?

Forward planning

Donald dreams of an encounter that is complete in itself. Shared agendas, agreed aims. Total resolution. He just can't switch off from work.

Liam always wakes up before the ending.

However, life is not generally like that, is it? Usually there are loose ends to tie up, and in any case healthcare plans should look forward. For example, Kerry-Ann's smoking is an important issue which may have been sidelined by other business on this occasion, but which should perhaps be addressed in the near future. The forward plan, like the plan made earlier in the interview, should be mutually acceptable. If the client or patient doesn't agree with it, nothing will be achieved. Thus the skills of negotiation come into play once again.

Dr Strait made a rocky start, but Kerry-Ann appreciates that he did make more of an effort as time went on. Therefore she might feel inclined to go to his new-patient clinic with Sister O'Mercy, even though it's not exactly top of her priority list at the moment.

You scratch my back and I might scratch yours.

The forward plan should address the following:

*   unfinished business (including 'safety net')
*   continuing problems (which did not surface during this interview)
*   risk factors (health promotion).

Kerry-Ann's unfinished business includes the question of whether or not she is pregnant. Dr Strait thinks it's unlikely, given her history, but there is a potential banana skin to be avoided. I have seen a girl who complained of constipation and, when examined, turned out to have an obvious 20-week-sized uterus. She was quite incredulous, having had a negative pregnancy test soon after her first missed period. Thus the timing of any test and the advisability of a repeat if negative results are obtained should be part of what Neighbour calls a *safety net* (*see* Chapter 2).[1]

Continuing problems are chronic conditions (such as asthma, diabetes mellitus or, in Kerry-Ann's case, acne) or situations (such as poor housing). Negotiating skills are sometimes necessary in order to 'sell' the advisability of action for conditions which are not causing problems at the present moment.

Risk factors are perhaps even more remote from the patient's or client's point of view. The threat of cancer or heart disease in middle age can be difficult for a young person to take seriously ('Hope I die before I get old' syndrome). Even older people have a tremendous capacity for denial (Uncle Fred smoked 40 a day and lived to be a 100). The 'you scratch my back and I'll scratch yours' mechanism is unlikely to be powerful enough to lead to long-term lifestyle changes.

'I'll give up smoking because you're such a nice man.' I don't think so.

Here are two techniques which *are* worthwhile in health promotion:

*   use their agenda
*   use cognitive dissonance.

Remember the salesman again (*see* Chapter 1). He tried to find out things about Fred that might be useful when persuading him to spend more money than he had orginally intended. A larger car was not on Fred's agenda, but his wife's good opinion of him (after he had failed to get a promotion) definitely was. The salesman played on this by using the idea of prestige associated with a larger and more expensive car. Wicked, don't you think?

Stopping smoking is not on Kerry-Ann's agenda. Cigarettes help her to feel 'cool' when she's out. They also help to relieve stress, and she has plenty of that at the moment. So what might there be, on Kerry-Ann's agenda, that could help the 'salesman' in Dr Strait or in Sister O'Mercy? Well, many young people are obsessed with their own body image and their acceptability to the opposite sex. They find this much more riveting than gambler's odds of their developing lung cancer in their fifties.

Kerry-Ann is much more likely to be interested in halitosis or in being able to exercise without getting out of breath. There's the hook for your health promotion salesperson. Smoking makes you sexually unattractive. Of course, it needs to be a little more subtle than that.

> Sister O'Mercy: 'What does your (non-smoking) boyfriend think about your smelling of fag smoke, dearie?'

Still not very subtle, is it? Especially the 'dearie'!
I'm sure you can think of different approaches that might work better.
I quite like Sister Brasstoff's 'straight from the shoulder' approach: 'You take it from me, lass. Men don't like their women smelling of ashtrays!'
Cognitive dissonance is a lovely piece of jargon. Literally, it means thoughts clashing. The theory is that your mind strives constantly for consistency (consonance), and tries to integrate any new information or thoughts with the existing structure (e.g. Uncle Fred smoked and lived a long time – therefore smoking is safe for me). If the integration is difficult, we have two choices:

- to change the existing structure to accommodate the new information (learning)
- to reject or ignore the new information (denial).

The denial mechanism is often robust and comes into operation quickly. One way round this 'force field' is to present the information at lightning speed, in a disguised form. An *awareness-raising question* is often very effective in this respect.

> Dr Strait: 'Do you actually *enjoy* smoking, Kerry-Ann?'

What's happening here?
For a split second, Kerry-Ann's defence mechanisms are experiencing difficulties. She would have been ready for a boring lecture (just switch off until the old gas bag has finished). But suddenly she's focusing on this idea that *she doesn't enjoy smoking that much*. So why does she do it, then? Could it be addiction? This is an acceptable thought. Having a good body and being attractive do not go with that. Actually, Sister O'Mercy also used an awareness-raising question. Did you notice that it was a combination of both techniques?

Probably she will survive that sudden loss of power in the deflector shield, but perhaps a seed has been sown that will weaken it in the longer term. Where is my evidence for this proposition? It's a fair cop, gov'. Perhaps I just like playing mind games with my patients.

Is it fair to use the other person's agenda or to assault their integrity by the technique of cognitive dissonance? Is all fair in health and war? Provided that it's for the patient's good?

Respect the autonomy of the other person.

Try to bear this in mind. It might keep you on the straight and narrow in a territory where the answers aren't obvious.

EXERCISE

Review your tape again, this time for presentation and forward planning skills.

Make a list of priorities.

Practise the skills.

Make another tape.

Repeat the cycle as necessary.

Is there hope for Dr Strait (or Sister Brasstoff)?

Will Kerry-Ann live to cough another day? Will Donald be riddled with bullet points? Will Liam care?

Between you and me, we're going to pack old Strait off to his local GP tutor and suggest that he includes communication skills in his personal learning plan. I expect that the tutor will point out that just reading and thinking about it isn't anywhere near enough. What Strait must do is to use his experiences in clinical practice as material for learning. Using a video recorder and following the exercises in this Chapter would help him. It would also help if he kept a notebook, diary or portfolio to keep track of his progress. Yes, the good doctor and all the members of the primary healthcare team must become *reflective practitioners* (*see* Chapter 10).

Returning to the *face* model, this Chapter has been about the skills needed to reconcile the agendas of the client and professional in order to devise and carry out a mutually acceptable plan (the central inverted triangle or 'nose'). The plan must relate to both agendas, particularly the client's, otherwise there is little hope of its coming to fruition.

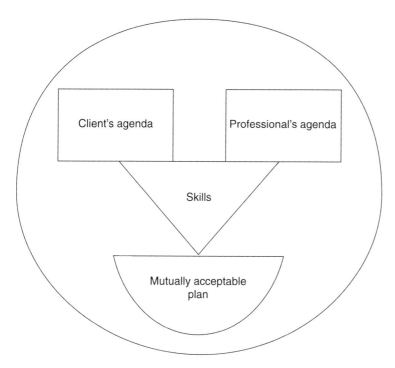

Figure 3.6

So far, to Donald's relief, we have skated over the area of emotions and feelings. The good news (for Liam) is that they have the next chapter all to themselves.

You could forgive Dr Strait and Sister Brasstoff for being a little confused by all the exhortations and advice they've received in this chapter on skills. Everyone has their own ideas about the parts and stages of an interview. Also the components keep getting mixed up, or arranged in the wrong order, and some of the skills seem to overlap. It is all very difficult for a tidy mind like Donald's. I'm going to suggest that they try some of the references in the Bibliography, particularly Neighbour's book on the consultation[1] and the book by Silverman, Kurtz and Draper.[8]

Finally, it might be helpful to lift out some of the key concepts (as I see them), in order to restore some shape to the chapter we have just completed.

You can do it

It's a question of attitude. Remember the following points:

- be friendly
- respect the other person
- want to do it (especially connecting with the other person's agenda)

- communication is risky (but it's worth it)
- negotiate the meaning, the situation and the roles
- the hands and feet are the main 'lie detectors'
- information-gathering (rapport, facilitation, clarification)
- processing (self-awareness, negotiation, management)
- concluding (presentation, forward planning).

Key skills

These include the following:

- open and closed questions
- attending behaviour and minimal encouragers
- lowering barriers
- paraphrasing
- reflecting feelings (but *see* Chapter 4)
- concreteness
- summarisation
- housekeeping
- negotiating
- prioritising
- safety-netting
- persuasion
- awareness-raising questions.

Add to this list if you like. After all, it's your book.

Liam has already scribbled all over his. Donald's looks like new. Can he *face* his feelings?
   We'll find out in the next chapter.

CHAPTER FOUR

That sixth sense
FEELINGS

'That means *feelings*. Yum!' says Liam.

'Yeouch!' says Donald, 'Anyway, everybody knows there are only five senses.'

'You're forgetting the pineal gland', says Liam, 'and haven't you heard of ESP?'

'What's that?' says Donald, 'Early summative profile?'

'You failed that at birth', says Liam.

You want to know about feelings? Try watching '*Neighbours*'. People talk about them all the time. They even talk about '*ageendas*'. Take it from me, this would not be usual in Loughborough (or especially in Shepshed). I don't know if it would be the same in real-life Australia, as opposed to the 'soaps'. Where I come from, the average male tends not to exhibit feelings. I blame the Viking hordes – when you're busy looting and pillaging, you can't afford to stray high up Maslow's hierarchy of needs.

We English are such a repressed lot, aren't we? However, we health professionals can be even more so. It's all to do with *professionalism*, you see. Distancing yourself.

There appear to be marked differences in approaches to education, at least in the early stages, by the nursing and medical professions. The former tends to be more holistic and the latter mainly disease-orientated. The nursing texts tend to emphasise the maturity of the trained nurse in relationships with their patients, meaning that the relationship is not exploited by the professional for their own needs. In the social science domain, Carl Rogers referred to 'non-possessive caring'.[1] Doctors are perhaps more concerned with the dangers of 'over-involvement' and the possibility of emotional issues clouding clinical judgements. The emotional maturity of the doctor does not seem to be much discussed, even though the transition from medical school and residence in hospital to the world outside is somewhat belated and abrupt.

> **THINK BOX**
>
> Where do you stand with regard to the position of involvement or distancing in relation to your patients or clients?
>
> Can you really be of any use to them, as a member of a caring profession, if you maintain a professional barrier?
>
> Should clients or patients relate to you primarily as another person, or as a professional wearing a badge of office (such as a uniform or a stethoscope)?
>
> If you favour more of a barrier, who are you protecting primarily – the clients or patients or yourself?
>
> Why?
>
> What problems have you encountered due to over-involvement?
>
> What problems have you encountered due to under-involvement?
>
> Where do you stand right now on the maturity scale?
>
> How much do you need your patients or clients?
>
> Have there been changes in this respect over the years since you qualified?
>
> Do you envisage further changes?

Here comes a feeling!

Donald is turning a delicate shade of green. Liam is ready to wallow.

How do we know about feelings?

- Because we're having them ourselves.
- Because another person tells us about them.
- Because we infer them from the other person's behaviour.

'I'm feeling frightened and lonely', says Kerry-Ann.

Sister O'Mercy notices that her voice is unsteady and that she is wringing her hands. 'Ah, to be sure, that means emotion, so it does', says the Sister to herself.

Dr Strait is suddenly feeling very depressed. 'Why should that be?' says he to himself. There are three main possibilities (according to Freeling and Harris):[2]

- the feeling is entirely from oneself
- there is a similarity to the feelings of the other person
- the feeling entirely reflects the state of the other person.

Dr Strait might be depressed because of his home life or the state of the National Health Service, or because it is in his genes (he's a closet Celt). It could even be a virus. Everything's a virus these days, isn't it?

Kerry-Ann and the doctor might have a similar feeling of low mood, even though each of them has different causes of it. Most of us are depressed on Monday mornings. It's my on-call day, not that I'm expecting any sympathy.

On the other hand, Dr Strait's mental state could be completely normal. He may be so adept at tuning to the feelings of others that he is experiencing Kerry-Ann's feeling as if it came from himself.

I'm sorry, Donald, but the bullet points don't really work, do they? It's misleading to imply that the three categories above are clear-cut. You can't easily put the sources of feelings into separate boxes. Nevertheless, it often helps to bear the framework in mind when we notice feelings arising, apparently from ourselves.

How do I know?

It sounds easy when someone tells you about their feelings (unless you don't believe them), or when you recognise feelings in yourself, but what about the third bullet point, namely inferring feelings from behaviour.

Patients tell me that I look worried when I take their blood pressure, but that's just the expression I have when concentrating.

I know a patient who laughs when she's upset. Perhaps she also cries when she's pleased, but I can't confirm that.

Communication about feelings is risky with a capital 'R'. It is risky because the outward signs can be difficult or impossible to interpret, and it is also risky because you don't know what you're letting yourself in for.

'Call yourself a doctor? You killed my mother!'

'Excuse me, but who exactly was your mother?'

Solve that one, if you can, by making everyone a cup of tea, and placing the tissues at strategic points.

EXERCISE

Make a list of the feelings you encounter in yourself or in others during a session of clinical practice.

Which did you find the most difficult?

Why was that?

Okay, so I've made my point – the interpretation of others' feelings is rather a minefield. However, don't give up yet, because help is at hand. You may not be able to understand what is happening, but it's as plain as a pikestaff that *something* is.

How do I know that? *Things don't add up.* Look.

- Kerry-Ann is playing with her fingers.
- Dr Strait is stroking his nose.
- The Prime Minister is adjusting his tie.
- Cats are washing themselves assiduously.
- Birds are pecking the branches frenetically.

None of them need to do what they are doing with such concentration. *Displacement activity* is what the social scientists call it – that is something going on inside, a sign of inner conflict.

Feelings are not always connected with conflict, of course, but harmonious ones (such as pure joy) are unlikely to give rise to ambiguous body language. Occasionally, I have seen one of my partners in a state of delirious happiness – usually over a football result. I know I was right because he bought me a drink.

- That girl who laughs when she's upset.
- That girl who turns on the water works to get her own way.
- Watch her hands. She's got every other part of her body under control but them.

As in any type of communication, but particularly the sort which involves feelings, you have to take a risk. You might be completely 'off beam'. They might think you're stupid. However, it's just as likely that they're laying a smokescreen, and I've got news for you.

Health professionals are allowed to be stupid.

Put out a pseudopodium, but be prepared to withdraw it and try another tack. You can even say it for them:

'I'm probably being stupid, but I get the feeling that something is wrong, even though you're laughing.'

'No, no! There's nothing wrong. Everything is all right. I don't know how you can say that it isn't!'

'Well, I'm sure you're right and I'm just being silly. Would you like somewhere to put all those bits of tissue you've torn up?'

Actually, though, my sixth sense is well polished. You ask me how I know about others' feelings. I just do.

EXERCISE

Look through your video tape (if you haven't got one, why not borrow a camcorder from one of your colleagues? GP trainers usually have one).

Look for instances of interesting non-verbal behaviour by the client or patient.

What do you think was going on?

Speculate about the feelings of the client or patient (write down as many possibilities as you can).

Give reasons for your opinions.

Are you usually right?

Recently, I was shown a video of someone I know going for his first parachute jump. As the aircraft climbed higher and higher, with unreassuring shots of the disappearing ground (through the permanently open hatch) to the ubiquitous sound of rock music, the camera zoomed in on his face. He was petrified, with a smile on his face. How did I know he was scared (apart from the fact that he told me later)? It was because I suddenly realised that I was seeing my own face at the point of discovering that my wife had booked me in for a helicopter lesson on my birthday – also immortalised on video. The fixed grin of pure panic.

First, know thyself.

How am I feeling?

How nice of me to ask. No, really!

Have you ever tried giving an honest answer to the question 'how are you'? They don't want to know, do they? That's because it's not really a question but a 'stroke' (see Eric Berne's book, *Games People Play*),[3] as in 'you scratch my back and I'll scratch yours'. The proper answer is 'fine, how are you?', to which the final answer is 'fine'. That's one stroke each and then we can go on our respective ways with our emotional baggage undisturbed. Very English.

There's so much to do at work and at home that we are sometimes in danger of neglecting ourselves, by which I mean our *inner* selves. Perhaps health professionals are even worse than average in this respect. We are trained to put other people first. I'd give away my last square of chocolate (even if it was dark chocolate) to someone who needed it more, wouldn't you?

Well, I'm giving you permission to be completely decadent.

Tune to yourself.

Why is this so wicked? Why do we have even a trace of embarrassment about having emotions? With doctors, I suspect it starts in the dissecting-room in the first week of medical school. I won't go into all the things that happened to me, and in any case there are plenty of lurid stories doing the rounds. There may have been some educational value in learning anatomy, but my main impression is of an initiation ceremony. It was decidedly 'uncool' to admit to any feelings about the experience. Those who did usually left during the first term. This implicit imperative to 'bottle it up' was reinforced by expectations of long working hours and sleep deprivation. Paradoxically, whilst on 'automatic pilot' we were having to look after patients who had need of emotional support as well as our technical skills. Part of me still regards myself with pride as being 'as tough as old boots'.

THINK BOX

The equivalent of the dissecting-room, for nurses, might be attendance at post-mortem examinations or dealing with offensive body fluids. Social workers also have to learn to cope with the more distressing aspects of humanity.

Focus on what, for you, has been a potentially dehumanising experience in your training as a health professional.

How has it affected you?

How have you adapted to the experience?

In my view, it's unfortunate for patients and clients when so many of the professionals who are supposed to be caring for them have been emotionally stunted by their training. We are full members of the human race as well as health professionals. Perhaps you feel that you have been dragged down to the depths by having to focus on unpleasant experiences. Now let us scale the heights as well.

The cognitive domain often seems to be valued most highly in our very 'rational' world. There is not much feeling in 'value for money' or 'joined-up thinking' is there? 'Emotional' arguments and 'irrationality' of the female of the species are part of a negative stereotype which often attaches to the affective domain.

When you develop this argument further, it falls to pieces. The logical, cognitive parts of our mental processes are often performed better and much more quickly by computers. Artificial intelligence – that is, a machine that can learn from experience – is no longer exclusive to the realm of science fiction. The affective domain, not the cognitive one, is what makes us truly human.

In *Star Trek*, Captain Kirk repeatedly tried to explain to an uncomprehending Mr Spock (who was only half human) that feelings often produce creative solutions to problems that baffle the more cognitive Vulcan race.

Christians believe that Jesus is God made man – that is, totally God and also totally man. In John's Gospel, Jesus demonstrated his divinity by raising Lazarus from the dead. Before this event, something else interesting was reported. Jesus was brought the news that his friend Lazarus had already died. What happened next? God made man demonstrated that he was fully human.

Jesus wept. Emotions, you see.

Great art must rank among the highest of human achievements. The cave paintings in the Dordogne, Michelangelo's murals in the Sistine chapel, Rembrandt's self-portraits in old age, Picasso's weeping woman, Henry Moore's locking pieces, Liz Frink's horses, Leo Tolstoy's *War and Peace*, Fyodor Dostoyevsky's *Brothers Karamazov*, Bach's *St Matthew Passion*, Pierre Boulez conducting *Pelleas and Melisande* by Debussy, and John Tomlinson singing 'Wotan' in the *Ring* cycle are among the images, ideas and sounds that I carry around with me. Without the range of human emotion they would be meaningless – indeed, they would not have existed.

What makes the art great is the way in which it can resonate through different times and social contexts. It reflects the human condition, which is what you and I humble health professionals encounter every day of our working lives.

EXERCISE

Go back to your videotape.

Alternatively, look through some recent case-notes.

Try to identify moments when you experienced strong feelings during the interviews.

Were those feelings particularly concerned with you, or did they emanate from the other person?

How did you handle the feelings, and with what result?

THINK BOX

Think back over significant events in your life that have generated strong feelings.

Do you often think about them, or are they largely 'buried'?

Have any of those experiences been of use to you in your professional life?

John Sassall's life as a country doctor (although not his tragic end) was described almost poetically in Berger's book, *A Fortunate Man*.[4] Having been trained as a surgeon, Sassall found that illnesses in general practice are mixed up with human emotions and social problems (*plus ça change*). He threw himself wholeheartedly into this new field *and tried to understand himself as a mirror of the human condition*. Living with his imagination on every level, first his own, then the patient's (rather like the exercises I've asked you to do, using videotapes or case-notes), Sassall attempted to offer himself as *the universal man*, someone who could keep another personality company 'in its loneliness', the function of such *fraternity* being *recognition*. During this period of his life, Sassall read the works of Sigmund Freud, as a result of which he became impotent (Berger does not say whether this was permanent). Anyway, I think you will see that he was a man of extremes.

Of course, it is neither possible nor necessary for one health professional to have everyone else's emotions in full measure, just as no one would expect you to have had every single illness or experienced every social situation. To paraphrase Jean-Paul Sartre, the hell of it is that other people are 'other' (*existential anguish* is the technical term).[5] Nevertheless, I believe that you *can* go some of the way towards bridging the unbridgeable gap. A degree of fraternity and recognition should be possible. However, it helps if you have had a few lessons in the school of hard knocks. A trainee I knew (in the years before they became known as registrars) used to respond to difficult emotional problems in consultations by saying 'that's life'. It was true, but he hadn't been there yet. Since then he's definitely earned his spurs, and is probably much more use to his patients as a result.

Not only is it impossible to know what it is like for another person, but any implication that you *do* know might be interpreted as insulting.

'I know just how you feel, dearie', says Sister O'Mercy.

Most of the patients forgive her because they can see that she's such a lovely person. Nevertheless, it is always best to allow the other person to be a unique individual, and not try to usurp their own experiences.

Respect the other person.

This is central to all forms of communication (as we have already seen in Chapter 3).

THINK BOX

Think of one work of art that has been of relevance to you as a health professional (mine is *The Death of Ivan Illych* by Leo Tolstoy).

What have you learned from it?

Another very powerful (and enjoyable) way to learn about feelings and all aspects of the human condition is to study the arts. For example, morbid jealousy is a problem I have certainly encountered in clinical practice. Flaubert's *Madame Bovary*, Zola's *Nana*, Tolstoy's *Anna Karenina* and Proust's *Remembrance of Things Past* all contain vivid accounts of it. *The Death of Ivan Illych*, as the title suggests, is a short story that deals with the issues surrounding dying and bereavement.

OPTIONAL EXERCISE

Listen to Barber's *Adagio for Strings* or the first movement of Elgar's *Cello Concerto*.

Contemplate one of Rembrandt's self-portraits (preferably the real thing, but a good print would do).

Contemplate Damien Hurst's *Mother and Child Divided*.

Read a favourite poem aloud.

If you can't empathise with any of my choices, substitute some of your own.

What do you gain from each of these experiences in emotional terms?

All of your life experiences, and the bells that are rung inside you by the arts, are grist to the mill. 'Being there' for another person as another human being who has lived, rejoiced and suffered is often all you can do, but it is enough.

To be able to use your own self, you must first tune to yourself.

Feel it for me

I hope Donald will forgive the *double entendre* in this line from a classic 'blues' song.

All right, Liam, I *know* I've already said that it's impossible to have someone else's experiences. Just trust me, OK? I'm talking about empathy, sympathy and 'the flash'.

Empathy is the skill of being able to put yourself mentally in the other person's shoes, even if just for a moment. Obviously you can't do it, although some health professionals may kid themselves that they can. Maybe you can't even come anywhere near 100 miles of it. Well, all we're doing is guessing what it might be like for the other person. Does that help? Well it *seems* to (no, Donald, I can't give you confidence limits on that one). Perhaps the more you've lived, and the more in tune you are with yourself, the better your guesses are likely to be.

Dr Strait achieved some empathy with Kerry-Ann when he thought of his own teenage daughter and how she might have felt in a similar situation. The main effect seemed to be a change in his own attitude towards the patient, so perhaps the accuracy of his guesses was not the point after all.

You could see empathy as being equivalent to making a diagnosis, in emotional terms. If empathy is a diagnosis, then *sympathy* is a treatment (according to Freeling and Harris).[2] We all know what sympathy is like, don't we? Usually nauseating, isn't it? Why *is* that? Because the empathy bit hasn't been done properly if at all. Therefore it is inappropriate and insensitive – it misses the point.

'Never mind', says Sister Brasstoff, 'Pretty girl like you. You'll find another man worth three of him.'

You wouldn't give treatment before you'd made a diagnosis, would you? No, your Honour!

My feeling is that you can pretty well dispense with sympathy, so long as you attend to respect for the other person.

The flash is a term coined by the psychoanalyst, Michael Balint, who described an intense experience *like a curtain rising*, which results in a new understanding of the other person's situation, which is different in degree from empathy.[6] It also results in the other person being aware of the scale of recognition that has taken place, and consequently a permanent change in the relationship between professional and client. The experience seems to be uncommon, and perhaps even rare. I think it has happened to me once or twice in 20 years. You could argue that tuning to yourself and achieving more accurate empathy would make 'the flash' more likely to happen. However, that doesn't seem to have happened for me.

I used to know a man who seemed to be a bit of a malingerer – he was frequently off work with a bad back, drawing it out until the last possible moment. One day I discovered that he had a handicapped teenage son who he didn't talk about, and for whom he refused all offers of practical help. His back injuries and their slow recovery were due to having to lift his son, and his own ageing process. My feelings towards him changed instantly and he knew it. That felt like a 'flash', although it was caused by my accidentally discovering some new information, rather than by my finely tuned sense of empathy. (So my database did leave something to be desired!)

EXERCISE

Review your audio or (preferably) video tape, or your case-notes.

Look for examples of empathy and sympathy.

How appropriate was your sympathy?

What effect did it seem to have?

Watch out! Emotions are about!

'Help!', says Donald, 'You've shown me how to release all these feelings. Now what *do* I do with them?'

'You can borrow my copies of the complete works of Freud, if you like', says Liam.

Many people think Sigmund Freud is old hat these days, especially since Karl Popper dismissed his work as unfalsifiable and therefore unscientific. This is also true of anything that deals with the inner workings of the mind, as opposed to the measurable behaviour that results from it. In terms of the human mind, any behaviour can mean its opposite (maddening, isn't it, Donald?). I can only 'know' the meaning of my patient's smiling (when she is upset) by experience of her, and ultimately by what she says. I can choose to believe her or not. Science is not the 'be all and end all' when it comes to understanding what makes people 'tick'.

Admittedly, psychoanalysis is not based on good science, but the *psychodynamic model* seems to me to be useful when considering the feelings side of communication. Freud postulated three divisions of the mind.[7] The *super-ego* is an internal parent or conscience, the *ego* is the logical (cognitive) self which integrates internal and external realities, and the *id* represents the desires of the physical organism. The model is, of course, hypothetical, and feelings are not identical with any one part of it. Nevertheless, the notion that the forces of the *id* obey the *pleasure principle* (rather than the reality principle) seems to describe the way in which feelings behave. These forces ignore the rules of logic and seek only for discharge, or to be released. Feelings 'well up', often over a prolonged time period. Even years later, when the person has 'got over it', some small thing may trigger the symptoms all over again, as if the memory traces have only been temporarily buried.

How does that help Kerry-Ann's boyfriend to deal with her when she returns home at the weekend? She keeps crying and going over the same things. He can't understand why this is necessary after he's listened to it at least three times. Dwelling on problems that you can't solve is only likely to make things worse, isn't it doctor?

At least Dr Strait's wife knows that *it's valuable just to listen, to be there as another human being.* The trouble is that she needs a break from it, before she cracks up herself. She thinks her husband should take early retirement.

When you're dealing with feelings:

* being there is enough – you don't have to solve the insoluble
* share the burden – many ears make light work
* help them to feel 'recognised' (empathy).

Delegation to other members of the team, including counsellors where available, or to friends, relatives and other carers (so long as you have explained what to expect), helps to protect everyone from burning out. Listening or 'being there' is helpful in itself, but being understood (even imperfectly) is better. The ability to use empathy (which is in turn dependent on the ability to be self-aware) is important here. Often the less that is said the better. Explaining and attempting to rationalise feelings is a waste of effort. Minimal encouragers and attending behaviour (see Chapter 3) are useful in promoting the discharge of feelings, or *catharsis*. Releasing the pressure helps, but the treatment usually needs much repetition. Permission to express feelings in a supportive atmosphere is often needed. The health professional should avoid showing embarrassment. Having paper tissues discreetly available and adopting a relaxed listening mode are usually sufficient.

In a health professional, being embarrassed about feelings is often the result of apparent powerlessness to solve the problems for the client. I repeat that you do not have to solve insoluble problems, but just to be there and recognise the other suffering human being. This may require more time than is commonly available in the doctor's or practice nurse's appointment, in which case you can bring the patient or client back, possibly involving another member of the team.

Safety net

Don't forget to ask yourself the following questions:

- Is this person depressed?
- Is there a risk of self-harm?

The bereavement model

'Why can't we have something more cheerful?', says Liam. 'This Chapter seems to be full of bad feelings.'

'I can tell you why that is', says Donald. 'Life is full of disappointments – in fact, life is one big disappointment.'

'Give me a tenner', says Liam, 'and I promise not to tell your wife you said so!'

Health professionals often deal with people who are unhappy with their lot. Perhaps that is why we need more holidays. I know there are exceptions – people who actually cheer you up, often through their positive approach to adversity, or because of what they say to you. A lady who hadn't seen me for years came in with a big smile on her face and told me I hadn't changed a bit, and that if anything I looked younger. To be honest, she had run out of her repeat prescription on a Saturday, but it's not often I receive compliments like that.

Life is difficult for all of us at one time or another. As the clock ticks on, more and more parts of us begin to hurt or wear out. Minor and major catastrophies impact on us or the people we care about – the 'slings and arrows of misfortune'. Health professionals are perhaps more able to see this as a normal part of life, but many of our clients or patients do not appear to expect that these things will happen.

'Life's a bitch and then you die' – try saying this with a smile on your face.

'Hail, holy Queen, mother of mercy....to thee do we send up our sighs, mourning and weeping in this vale of tears.' Asking for divine help is one strategy which helps believers to cope with their problems.

Let us not forget that life is good, despite the difficulties. The happiest people are not always the ones with the fewest problems. Life *is* full of disappointments and we cope with them – some of us better than others. Each reverse we suffer is like a little bereavement which can prepare us for our own death.

Here is a simple version of the bereavement model:

- shock
- work
- reorientation.

Shock

Adverse events can be unexpected. I was once telephoned by a woman who told me only that her husband 'didn't look very well'. Not only was it obvious, when I arrived, that he was dead (and had been for some time), but his wife plainly did not believe this. Shock is maximal if the event is a complete surprise, and is usually much less when it is preceded by an opportunity for preparation, such as a prolonged terminal illness. Sometimes it seems as if relatives can experience their bereavement in advance of the death.

Denial is often a prominent feature of extreme shock (as in the case of the woman described above). Unacceptable facts are treated as if they do not exist. There is a strong parallel with *cognitive dissonance* (*see* Chapter 3). It can often feel as if input to the conscious part of our minds has been partially shut down.

'I can't feel anything.'

'It's like being surrounded by cotton wool.'

This may make the bereaved feel guilty. Someone they love has just died, and they can't even cry. You and I know that this is quite normal, but the relatives may need permission not to feel anything for now.

Work

Now the trouble starts.

As the shock begins to wear off, all of the feelings start to flood in. By now, a few weeks may have passed, and those who haven't yet experienced any hard knocks may think that the bereaved person should be getting better. People cross to the other side of the street to avoid them. That makes them feel paranoid and isolated, but it is only because others are afraid of the situation and do not know what to say. They particularly dare not mention the event itself, or the person who has died, whereas the bereaved person would like to talk of nothing else. However, they won't, because they know that others can't handle it.

Sometimes it seems as though the person they have lost is still with them. At times they can hear, smell and almost touch them. Maybe they have also seen them at night, but they won't tell anyone this. Do they have an immortal soul, or is denial taking hold of them again? Other people would think them mad if they told them such things. Perhaps this is how madness begins?

At other times, the memories seem to fade. The face of the person who has died is hard to visualise. They begin to idealise the image. *Anger* comes with the realisation of what they have lost. Perhaps they can focus it outside, on to someone to blame – for example, a health professional who seemed to fall short of the ideal.

'If that Dr Strait hadn't insisted on finishing his surgery, our Fred might still have been here.'

Anger which has no obvious outside target is often directed inwards as *guilt*.

'If only I'd been more sympathetic to his complaints. I should have made him go to the doctor earlier.'

Remember that feelings just well up, like a force obeying the 'pleasure principle'. It is useless to rationalise, or to reason with them. You have to keep going over the same ground until the force is lessened. This is called the *grief work*. Dreams are often full of it. This phase takes much longer than other people may think. Contact with others does help, provided that they know they must just listen and not try to solve the problem.

Reorientation

Eventually, memories become more realistic, and even anger with the dead person can be worked through. The force of the well becomes less oppressive, allowing gradual reorientation to the outside world. New interests, projects and even relationships can be contemplated. However, the memories remain, and strong feelings may be triggered by what may to others appear to be trivial events.

In the case of a divorce, the long-awaited decree absolute (a formality in the eyes of others) may result in tears, although the relationship has long been acknowledged to be at an end.

Fortunately, the health professionals are well aware of all these problems connected with bereavement, and can explain what is happening, as well as offer support, to the patients and their relatives. They often need broad shoulders to be able to handle some of the anger, which may be unfair. It helps to realise that feelings behave like a force. There is nothing personal in the onslaught of the waters from a breached dam.

Bereavement is probably the most extreme form of the model, but it can be applied to any of the 'slings and arrows of life', such as serious illnesses, accidents, breakdown of relationships and business failure.

Face up to it

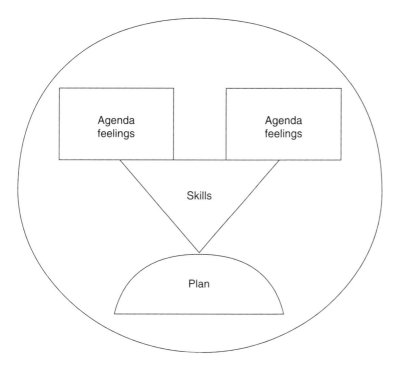

Figure 4.1

Feelings slot naturally into the *face model*. They belong with the agendas of each party. The skills needed to deal with feelings overlap with other communication skills, such as interpretation of verbal and non-verbal behaviour, facilitation and clarification. Of particular importance are self-awareness, catharsis, empathy (perhaps 'flash'), valuing feelings and giving permission for them to be expressed. The mutually agreed plan may include professional counselling, support by members of the primary healthcare team, or explanation of the role required of them to carers.

> Sister O'Mercy: 'Kerry-Ann, you seem rather agitated. You're making me feel quite sad. It's not just the sore throat, is it?'
> Kerry-Ann (putting her head down): 'N...no...I'm sorry.'
> Sister O'Mercy: 'It's all right to cry, my dear. Just imagine I'm your mother.'
> Kerry-Ann (sharply): 'But I *hate* my mother!'
> Sister O'Mercy: 'Then it wasn't a good choice of words I made, was it?'
> Kerry-Ann: 'That's just the kind of thing *she* would say. People of your age...you're all the same!'
> Sister O'Mercy: 'I'm really sorry. You're very upset, aren't you? You don't have to tell me if you don't want to.'

Kerry-Ann: 'No, it's me that should be sorry. It makes me so angry! It's not to do with you.'

Sister O'Mercy: 'To do with what, then?... Take your time.'

Kerry-Ann: 'My boyfriend at home – he just doesn't understand. Every time I try to tell him, he switches off – says it doesn't help to keep bringing it up.'

Sister O'Mercy: 'Bringing it up...'

Kerry-Ann: 'I had sex with someone else during freshers' week. I didn't even *know* him. And I feel so guilty and cheap... but it was all because I was lonely. He can't seem to see that.'

Sister O'Mercy: 'That must be difficult for your boyfriend to talk about. At least he's still there.'

Kerry-Ann: 'Yes, I can see I'm being selfish... but I can't think of anything else.'

Sister O'Mercy: 'Perhaps he's switching off because he doesn't know what to say to you?'

Kerry-Ann: 'But if only he knew... he doesn't have to say anything... just let me know if he cares.'

Sister O'Mercy: 'I know that, but he's only a boy, not a nurse or a doctor. You could try telling him what you've just told me.'

Kerry-Ann: 'Do you think it would work?'

Sister O'Mercy: 'You could try... Otherwise, bring him here with you, and I'll tell him.'

THINK BOX

What do you think of Sister O'Mercy's professionalism, and the skills she used?

How does it compare with some of your own experiences?

Feeling the way forward

Here is a summary of where we've been so far:

* distancing, over-involvement and maturity
* interpretation of feelings and their source
* skills and risks
* know yourself first
* feelings and the human condition – the arts
* respect for the other (again)
* recognition and fraternity
* empathy, sympathy and 'the flash'
* feelings as unreasoning force – catharsis

- sharing the burden
- watch out for depression
- the bereavement model for life
- back to the *face*.

For the professional, there is always a tightrope to walk between too much distance on the one hand, and over-involvement on the other. The mature health professional can use self-knowledge without exploiting the client or patient for their own gratification. *Respect for the other is the key*, as it is in other forms of communication.

It is necessary to monitor one's own behaviour constantly.

'Aren't we serious, all of a sudden?' says Liam.
'Quite right, too', says Donald.

Nurses have 'clinical supervision', in which they discuss these dilemmas with colleagues, who warn them if they appear to be getting over-involved with patients. However, doctors have so far convinced themselves that they do not need this, but times are changing. Watch out for Dr Avenger. He's the new 'clinical governor'.

In any case, some of the scenarios we have to cope with are very challenging indeed, but that subject will be dealt with in the next chapter.

CHAPTER FIVE

Challenging scenarios
DIFFICULT SITUATIONS

Liam: 'A doctor friend of mine was once called by the local CBU.'

Donald: 'What's the CBU?'

Liam: 'I thought *everyone* knew that, Donald. CBU stands for Challenging Behaviour Unit, of course. Well, anyway, my friend rings the person in charge and asks "what's the problem?" '

Donald: 'What was the problem?'

Liam: 'Challenging behaviour.'

Donald: 'What did they mean "challenging behaviour"? Didn't you say it was a Challenging Behaviour Unit?'

Liam: 'That's just what he said.'

Donald: 'So what did they say?'

Liam: 'They said the behaviour had got *more* challenging.'

Donald: 'I'm glad I stuck with boring old accountancy.'

For health professionals, every encounter is potentially challenging. It is just that some are rather more challenging than others. However, exactly the same principles apply as in more ordinary situations (*see* Chapters 3 and 4).

A young and athletic-looking man once walked into my consulting room, sat down in my chair and started tapping at random on the computer keyboard. Fixing me with a stare, he announced: 'I *am* the revelation, and the only way I can gain my freedom is by killing *you*.'

I've just said that the same general principles that are relevant to ordinary consultations apply in this kind of situation as well. The trouble is that your adrenaline starts to flow and you are aware of your pulse beating at a much faster rate than usual. It helps if you know the procedure by heart. Like a true 'pro', I followed the *face* model. My colleagues (who are a heartless lot) fell about laughing when I told them what I said in reply.

'How can I help you?'

You think I'm making this up, don't you? Well perhaps I am, but here is a tip. People who are truly mad don't have a coherent agenda, so when you ask them what comes next, it tends to floor them. That leaves you in charge to organise it for them – that is, an ambulance and some men in white coats.

In the examples that follow, remember the *face* model.

Figure 5.1

As the health professional, you are there to use your skills to help the other person. That's the key to it.

So demanding

Sister O'Mercy has just finished her clinic one evening, and is tidying up her equipment in the treatment room. Suddenly, a man bursts through the door unannounced.

> Mr Threepiece: 'This is ridiculous. All I need is for you to syringe my ears, but that *woman* out there says I have to see the doctor and maybe put drops in my ears for a week, first!'
>
> Sister O'Mercy: 'That must be difficult for you, if you can't hear very well. Why don't you sit down? What job do you do, then?'

Mr Threepiece: 'I'm a sales manager.'

Sister O'Mercy: 'You'll be spending a lot of time on the telephone, so you will?'

Mr Threepiece: 'That's just the point. It's making my job impossible.'

Sister O'Mercy: 'Well, I was supposed to have finished, and there are reasons for what the manager said, but I'll help you if I can.'

Mr Threepiece: 'Thank you, nurse. I'm sorry to have burst in on you like that.'

Sister O'Mercy: 'That's all right, dear. Now let me just explain it to you. It might well be wax in your ears, like you say, but there are other possibilities which might be made worse by syringing.'

Mr Threepiece: 'What sort of possibilities?'

Sister O'Mercy: 'Well there could be an infection, or even a perforated ear-drum. You wouldn't want your ear syringing in that case, would you?'

Mr Threepiece: 'Wouldn't I have pain, if that were the case?'

Sister O'Mercy: 'Not necessarily, but anyway, if I speak to the duty doctor nicely, he might have a little look for you.'

Mr Threepiece: 'That would be marvellous. Then do you think I could have my ears syringed?'

Sister O'Mercy: 'If there's wax, it's usually too hard to get out in one go. Then it's best to wait a few days and put the drops in.'

Mr Threepiece: 'Yes, I suppose you're right, although it will make it almost impossible for me at work. Thank you – you've been very kind.'

THINK BOX

Could you see the *face* model in action?

What do you think might have happened if Sister O'Mercy had taken a different line (invent some scenarios)?

Can you think of some situations with demanding clients in your practice?

How did you handle them?

What was the outcome?

Would you do the same again?

If not, what would you do instead?

Angry

Mrs Whiplash had a car accident almost a year ago. Her neck still hurts and her claim for compensation against the other driver continues to drag on. Now her solicitor has told her that the doctor is delaying things by refusing to release the medical records, except for an exorbitant fee.

Dr Shorts: 'Do come in, Mrs Whiplash. Have a seat. How are you, then?'

Mrs Whiplash (slamming the door and putting her bag heavily on the desk): 'I don't know how you can ask me that, when you're the cause of the trouble!'

Dr Shorts: 'Me, causing you trouble?'

Mrs Whiplash (her voice unsteady and rising in volume): 'I can't believe that you pretend to know nothing about it... it's obviously of no importance to you! I'm just wasting my time and breath! (She rises from her chair). Well, you'll be sorry when I've complained to the health authority!'

Dr Shorts: 'I'm really sorry you're angry, and I'd like to help if I can.'

Mrs Whiplash: 'Don't try to tell me that you haven't had a letter from my solicitor, asking you to release the notes.'

Dr Shorts: 'Yes, I've had a letter.'

Mrs Whiplash: 'And you've had my written permission?'

Dr Shorts: 'Yes.'

Mrs Whiplash (angrily): 'Then why can't you send them as you've been requested? My solicitor said you wanted a hundred and twenty pounds. Quite ridiculous!'

Dr Shorts: 'I'm not trying to make money out of you, Mrs Whiplash.'

Mrs Whiplash: 'Why are you asking so much, then? (she falters and sits down). It's making me bad, all this is. My neck hurts every day. I'm sure it's getting worse (she takes out a handkerchief). All this because of an idiot who didn't look in front of him!'

Dr Shorts: 'Dear, dear. I can see you're in a state, and it's not surprising. It's unfair when someone drives into the back of your car, and you've done nothing to deserve it.'

Mrs Whiplash nods her head in agreement.

Dr Shorts: 'And now it must seem as though everyone is against you, even your doctors.'

Mrs Whiplash: 'Well, what *am* I to think? Anyway, I don't particularly care about the money. I just want to be normal again. Do you think I ever will be?'

Dr Shorts: 'People often have pain from this sort of injury for more than a year, but they usually recover. The specialist said there is no reason why you shouldn't.'

Mrs Whiplash: 'I know he said that, but it does feel as though it might go on for ever.'

Dr Shorts: 'Well, because there's a lot of muscle spasm involved in cases like this, it does tend to get worse when you're anxious or worried – for example, when there are legal things hanging over.'

Mrs Whiplash: 'Yes, it feels like that. So why can't you help me a bit more with these medical records?'

Dr Shorts: 'I will try and sort things out with your solicitor. Perhaps I'll phone him up. I'm afraid they sometimes play games with us, to see if they can get things for a reduced fee – even though the money will come from the other driver's insurance, assuming you win the case. Since you weren't at fault, I assume there'll be no problem with that?'

Mrs Whiplash: 'No, I suppose not, though it all seems to be taking so much time. It makes me feel as if I'm the guilty party at times. Still, you must admit that a hundred and twenty pounds does sound a lot, just to send some records.'

Dr Shorts: 'I'll try and explain it to you. First of all, this sort of work is outside our contract with the National Health Service.'

Mrs Whiplash: 'Yes, I realise that.'

Dr Shorts: 'Well, we can't just send the notes because we need them here. Not everything is on the computer yet. Also, we get a lot of requests like this from solicitors, for all sorts of reasons. We'd have real problems if we let all the notes go, for goodness knows how long. Solicitors used to ask us for reports from the notes, but now they always want the whole of medical records for one of their own medical experts to go through. So we have to photocopy everything.'

Mrs Whiplash: 'That sounds like a lot of work for someone.'

Dr Shorts: 'The staff hate doing it, and of course, we have to pay for their extra hours, not to mention wear and tear of the machinery. Here, look at the size of your notes!'

Mrs Whiplash: 'I didn't realise so much was written about me.'

Dr Shorts: 'Most people's notes are like this nowadays. Everyone has to write more, for legal reasons, and nothing can be thrown away. What's more, *I* have to read through the whole lot, before we can let the photocopies go out.'

Mrs Whiplash: 'Why is that?'

Dr Shorts: 'You never know what might be in the notes. They go right back to your birth, you know. Sometimes there are things written about other people, usually before doctors had to be as careful as they are now. Also, there might be something there about yourself, that you've forgotten, and that you wouldn't like to go outside the surgery. If I saw something like that, I'd want to discuss it with you first.'

Mrs Whiplash: 'I can't imagine that there'd be anything like that in my notes, but I can see why you have to look. It must take a lot of your time.'

Dr Shorts: 'It's certainly not my favourite job, and my time isn't cheap on BMA rates. Still, I think you'll find that it's a lot less than your solicitor charges per hour.'

Mrs Whiplash: 'So you're saying that it's a bit rich, my solicitor complaining about your fees?'

Dr Shorts: 'That's right, but you're welcome to check it out. Anyway, I said I'd try and help, and I will. I'll phone your solicitor today, and try and come to an understanding with him. I don't think he realises how poorly the delay is making you.'

Mrs Whiplash: 'Thank you, doctor. I'd be really grateful.'

THINK BOX

Can you identify the skills used by Dr Shorts and how they fit in with the *face* model?

Think of an angry patient or client you have encountered recently.

How did you handle the anger?

What was the result?

Would you change anything, in retrospect?

Did you get angry, too?

How did that influence the outcome?

When you're scared or angry, the adrenaline starts to pump, and that has physical effects on you which are difficult to control (for example, the volume and pitch of your voice). To defuse the situation, it helps to *listen* and to try to put yourself in the shoes of the other person – in other words, to *empathise*. The previous two chapters dealt in more detail with the skills that you might use. Concentrating on the other person's needs helps to dissipate any anger that you might feel in reaction, and your protagonist will be mollified by getting the message that *you're on their side*. Later on, you can explain the relevant parts of your own agenda and negotiate with them.

If you are unsuccessful in defusing their anger, the situation could deteriorate into violence. Usually there are ample warnings of this, particularly non-verbal signs such as staring, shouting and a threatening posture. You might need to adopt a defensive but non-threatening stance (side-on with arms raised and hands spread out). Risky locations and situations in your working environment are worth considering as a preventive measure. Self-defence and risk management are beyond the remit of this book. It is best to defuse the situation, and you almost always can do this.

Complaining

Dr Strait has received a letter of complaint about one of the practice nurses, Sister Brasstoff, from Mr Pickett, who attends their clinic for dressings of his leg ulcer. According to the patient, Sister Brasstoff was rude to him. Allegedly, she 'told him off for being one minute late', and proceeded to punish him by dealing very roughly with his dressing. Dr Strait has already interviewed Sister Brasstoff, who admitted that she was 'a bit grumpy with him because he was 10 minutes late', but denied any unprofessional behaviour. She also intimated suspicion about the length of time it was taking for the ulcer to heal. 'Something didn't add up there', she said.

> Dr Strait: 'Well, Mr Pickett, I've read your letter of complaint carefully and I've also interviewed Sister Brasstoff.'

Mr Pickett: 'So what are you going to do about it, Dr Strait?'

Dr Strait: 'Well, it's always difficult to know exactly what happened, not having been a fly on the wall. Sister Brasstoff's perception of events is not quite the same as yours, as you can probably imagine.'

Mr Pickett: 'Are you saying that I'm not telling the truth?'

Dr Strait: 'No, I'm not saying that. I'm not saying that about either of you.'

Mr Pickett: 'What *are* you saying, then?'

Dr Strait: 'I'm saying that people have their own perceptions, and they're true for *them*. However, I'm not trying to "fudge" the issue. I'm here to try and help. The object is to improve the service we give you.'

Mr Pickett: 'How will you do that?'

Dr Strait: 'For a start, I'm sure Sister Brasstoff will think hard about the talk we've had, and try to avoid any more complaints like the one you've made.'

Mr Pickett: 'Is that all?'

Dr Strait: 'There are some other things we could look at in the area of practice organisation. The nurses are very pushed for time, you know. Sometimes it's harder to get to see the nurse than it is to see me. If they felt less under pressure, they might not mind so much if patients were a little bit late.'

Mr Pickett: 'It wasn't my fault I was late. The bus was held up.'

Dr Strait: 'Yes, I know these things happen. We do try to keep to time here, though, and it helps us enormously if people turn up slightly early.'

Mr Pickett: 'Mmm...'

Dr Strait: 'What else did you want to happen, as a result of this complaint?'

Mr Pickett: 'I just wanted to make sure that she had more respect for people in future.'

Dr Strait: 'Are you reasonably happy that I've dealt with it under the practice complaints procedure, or were you thinking of taking it further?'

Mr Pickett: 'It depends whether she takes notice.'

Dr Strait: 'I think she has taken your complaint very seriously, but maybe you should make some allowances as well? It's hardly a "sacking" offence, is it? You don't seem to have come to any harm.'

Mr Pickett: 'No, but my ulcer's taking a long while to get better.'

Dr Strait: 'Well, you've had first-class care from the nurses. I think it might be time to reassess the situation from the medical point of view – maybe even refer you to a specialist.'

THINK BOX

How do you think Mr Pickett felt after his interview with Dr Strait?

Do you think Sister Brasstoff will take any notice?

How would you have handled that complaint?

To what extent do you think Dr Strait followed the *face* model?

Did it matter?

How do you feel about complaints against yourself? Are they jewels, or a personal affront?

Notice how the concept of *respect* is often important in a complaint (as in all communication). Perhaps the most important desired outcome, from Mr Pickett's point of view, is that he should be respected by the health professionals. Perhaps, in a case like this (where it sounds like 'six of one and half a dozen of the other'), neither side should be made to feel that they have 'lost face', but some positive plans should be put in place. For example, the practice might consider employing a phlebotomist to deal with the blood tests, in order to free up some of the nurse's time. On the other hand, if complaints about Sister Brasstoff's manner continue, the issue of her communication skills might need to be tackled.

I don't know how to tell you this

Mrs Fleming is a smoker in her mid-fifties with a persistent cough. She has come for the result of her chest X-ray, which is reported as showing 'an enlarged hilum, consistent with a bronchogenic carcinoma'.

Dr Shorts: 'Do sit down, Mrs Fleming. You've come for the result of your chest X-ray, haven't you?'

Mrs Fleming: 'Yes.'

Dr Shorts: 'Have you been worried about it?'

Mrs Fleming: 'Of course I have! Wouldn't you?'

Dr Shorts: 'What was going through your mind?'

Mrs Fleming: 'For Pete's sake, tell me the result!'

Dr Shorts (shifting uncomfortably in his seat): 'Well it doesn't look good...'

Mrs Fleming: 'It's cancer, isn't it?'

Dr Shorts: 'Well, I don't know for sure...'

Mrs Fleming: 'You can stop beating about the bush, doctor. I'm not a fool. I've smoked 20 a day for the last 40 years, and I know this cough has been getting worse. How long have I got?'

Dr Shorts: 'I don't know the answer to that. If I knew, I'd tell you. I don't even know whether it's definitely cancer. Shall I tell you what the report says?'

Mrs Fleming indicates that the doctor should go ahead. He reads the report to her. Breaking bad news is probably one of the most 'risky' situations in communication, in the sense that one has to test the water and be prepared to try another tack. The importance of finding out 'where the other person is coming from', and what they want from you, cannot be over-emphasised.

THINK BOX

Why was Dr Shorts 'beating about the bush'?

Was it mainly for the patient's sake, or mainly for his own?

How would you have handled Mrs Fleming?

Why?

Let's pretend that Mrs Fleming is a simulated patient, which means that we can rewind the scene and try something different instead.

Dr Shorts: 'Do take a seat, Mrs Fleming. You've had a persistent cough and you've come for the result of your chest X-ray – is that right?'

Mrs Fleming: 'That's right, doctor.'

Dr Shorts: 'The report says that you need more investigation.'

Mrs Fleming: 'More investigation?'

Dr Shorts: 'Yes, because it looks as though something is enlarged in part of your lung.'

Mrs Fleming: 'Is it serious?'

Dr Shorts: 'It could be, yes.'

Mrs Fleming: 'Do you mean cancer, doctor?'

Dr Shorts: 'It could well be, but they don't know for sure.'

Mrs Fleming: 'I knew it was something serious. How long does it take, doctor?'

Dr Shorts: 'How long does it take...?'

Mrs Fleming: 'Yes, I mean I know they can't cure it. I'd like to be able to go and see my relatives in Canada.'

Dr Shorts: 'Well, we don't know if it is definitely cancer from this X-ray. Even if it is, there are different types and different people react to them in different ways. That's why you need more investigation.'

Mrs Fleming: 'Yes, I see.'

Dr Shorts: 'The investigations will tell us whether or not it is cancer, and what kind of treatment would be worth trying.'

Mrs Fleming: 'I didn't know you could treat it.'

Dr Shorts: 'They can usually do something, even if it isn't a cure.'

Mrs Fleming: 'How can they find out what to do?'

Dr Shorts: 'You'll have to go to a specialist, and you'll probably have to have an investigation called a bronchoscopy.'

Mrs Fleming: 'Is that one of those camera things?'

Dr Shorts: 'Yes. They do it under anaesthetic, of course, and they can look right down into your bronchial tubes, and take a sample if they need to.'

THINK BOX

Do you think the second way was better?

Why (or why not)?

How does that compare with what you would have done?

In each of the two scenarios described above, you can probably imagine that there would be gaps and pauses for information to sink in, with quite a variety of non-verbal communication as well (*see* Chapters 3 and 4). *Chunking and checking* is an important technique for giving information in amounts that can be easily assimilated. It is particularly useful when giving bad news, because the shock of hearing the first unwelcome item may prevent subsequent information from being registered.

- Give bad news in small degrees.
- Check for understanding.
- Respond to the other person's questions.

THINK BOX

Did Dr Shorts need to check for understanding?

If not, why not?

Do you think health professionals should always tell the truth when they have to give bad news?

If not, why not?

Could do better

Mrs Chocbox is one of the older receptionists, who used to be with Dr Strait before his practice became a group practice. She has a very friendly and extrovert personality, and is popular with many of the patients. However, Mrs Praisall, the new practice manager, has noticed that she is increasingly tending to give the patients advice, which often sounds patronising.

Mrs Praisall: 'I've made you a cup of tea, Ruby. I thought we might have a quick chat.'

Mrs Chocbox: 'What's it all about, Anne?'

Mrs Praisall: 'I'd like your help with the new "risk management" strategy that Dr Avenger wants us to introduce.'

Mrs Chocbox: 'Risk management?'

Mrs Praisall: 'Yes, it means looking for all the common things that go wrong in the organisation, and lead to mistakes or complaints.'

Mrs Chocbox: 'You mean like investigation results that are not followed up?'

Mrs Praisall: 'Yes, that's a good example, where we can tighten up our procedures and minimise the chances of anything going wrong.'

Mrs Chocbox: 'That makes sense.'

Mrs Praisall: 'Yes, it does, doesn't it? And since you're our most experienced receptionist, I'd like you to help me and give a lead to the others.'

Mrs Chocbox: 'Well, the organisation and administration isn't really my line, is it?'

Mrs Praisall: 'No, but dealing with patients at the desk and on the telephone is where you come into your own. You have such a wealth of experience. All the new receptionists look up to you.'

Mrs Chocbox: 'It's very nice of you to say so, Anne. I enjoy my job. I suppose you pick up all sorts of things when you've been doing it for years.'

Mrs Praisall: 'Well, we have to tighten up our procedures "on the desk" as well. Dr Avenger thinks we have to present a more professional front.'

Mrs Chocbox: 'What? Do you mean uniforms – that sort of thing?'

Mrs Praisall: 'Not necessarily, but I would like your opinion on that, too. The main thing, though, is what we actually say to patients.'

Mrs Chocbox: 'Yes, well, I can help you there. Patients like you to be friendly. I keep trying to help the newer receptionists have more confidence.'

Mrs Praisall: 'That's very good. I don't want us to lose that, but "risk management" means that we have to be much more careful about giving advice to patients.'

Mrs Chocbox: 'Advice? I've been doing that for years. When you know what they need, and if they can buy it from the chemist's without having to bother the doctor. That's more efficient, isn't it?'

Mrs Praisall: 'Well, it might be, but what if something goes wrong? You've had so much experience and I know your advice is probably sensible, but what if someone turned out to have a pneumonia when they'd been advised to get a cough linctus?'

Mrs Chocbox: 'I suppose it could happen, though it seems unlikely. You have a feeling when someone's really poorly.'

Mrs Praisall: 'The younger ones won't be half as good as you at telling. Anyway, the doctors get it wrong sometimes.'

Mrs Chocbox: 'That's true enough.'

Mrs Praisall: 'The point is that the doctors get the blame if we give advice and something goes wrong. Also, some patients don't like it if we ask them questions about their medical complaint.'

Mrs Chocbox: 'Is this called "progress"?'

Mrs Praisall: 'Everything's changed, I'm afraid. People are much more likely to complain if the slightest thing goes wrong.'

Mrs Chocbox: 'You can say that again. Still, I can see you can't go back to how it was in the old days.'

Mrs Praisall: 'That's very perceptive of you, Ruby. We're lucky to have someone with your years of experience who can still be adaptable to change.'

Mrs Chocbox: 'Oh, it's not the first set of changes I've been through.'

Mrs Praisall: 'That's why I'd like you to give some leadership on the new style of communication "at the desk".'

THINK BOX

Do you think Mrs Praisall did well?

Can you pinpoint the skills she was using?

How far did she follow the *face* model?

Is there anything she could have done better?

If so, what and why?

When does effective communication become manipulation?

How much does it matter?

An appraisal

Mrs Fishent is another of the practice's more senior receptionists. She is about to have her first annual appraisal meeting with the new young practice manager. As preparation for the meeting, the receptionist has been given a self-appraisal form to complete, and a written explanation of the procedure and its purpose.

Mrs Praisall: 'Elsie, you've had a chance to read the leaflet and fill out the self-appraisal form. Have you any questions about that?'

Mrs Fishent: 'It all seems very new. I know they do this sort of thing in industry, but this is not like manufacturing cars, is it?'

Mrs Praisall: 'Do you have some worries about the purpose of it?'

Mrs Fishent: 'Well, you're bound to, aren't you? I mean I've been doing this job a long time, and I think I'm good at it... and with all due respect, Anne, you haven't been here five minutes before all this comes along.'

Mrs Praisall: 'So you think I've brought appraisal with me from outside, and that I don't really know the situation in primary care well enough?'

Mrs Fishent: 'Well, I don't think you've ever been a doctor's receptionist, have you?'

Mrs Praisall: 'You're quite right, Elsie. There's a lot I need to learn about the details of the job you do. That's one reason for having this meeting, actually.'

Mrs Fishent: 'Are you saying that you really want to learn from me?'

Mrs Praisall: 'Yes, of course. You have to understand that appraisal is meant to be a two-way process. It's supposed to benefit both the individual and the organisation. Have you any other worries about it?'

Mrs Fishent: 'Yes. What happens to all the information? I suppose it goes into your files, does it?'

Mrs Praisall: 'We agree between the two of us, Elsie, about the content of the report. Nothing goes in it that you don't want. Then we both have to sign it, and you can have a copy to keep.'

Mrs Fishent: 'That sounds all very well in theory, but you could always write your own private version if you felt like it. Suppose I told you something, in this spirit of "mutual honesty" that the leaflet talks about, and I didn't want it in the report, but you felt obliged to use it, just the same?'

Mrs Praisall: 'I can assure you, Elsie, that this meeting is completely confidential. I can see why you might find it difficult to trust someone you don't know very well, who has been brought in from a management background. All I can say is that a good appraisal system overcomes these fears – which everybody has – in industry, where you might expect less grounds for trust than in a small business like this. Another thing is that I am not the one who is responsible for appraisal arriving in this practice. Dr Avenger is very keen on it and, if you look round the other practices in the area, most of them are already doing it. It's inevitable with the growth of practice development plans, and that's national policy.'

Mrs Fishent: 'What about you, Anne? Do you get appraised?'

Mrs Praisall: 'Yes, I've already had it done by Dr Strait.'

Mrs Fishent: 'We're a bit in the same boat, then, but what about Dr Strait? Who does him?' (she laughs, and so does Mrs Praisall).

Mrs Praisall: 'I daren't ask. Isn't it awful? Maybe it's someone at his club?'

Mrs Fishent: 'I was only joking!'

Mrs Praisall: 'It's a good point, though. Anyway, I can't expect everybody to feel completely comfortable with appraisal until it's been working for a while, until they see the benefits, and that it's nothing sinister.'

Mrs Fishent: 'You'll have to give us time, and I expect we'll all come round in the end.'

Mrs Praisall: 'I hope so. What it's really about is helping you to do your job better, so that we give a better service throughout the practice, all pulling together.'

Mrs Fishent: 'I admit that it sounds good.'

Mrs Praisall: 'It includes looking at problems that you might have because I'm not doing *my* job as well as I might. If I can, I'll put it right, but I can't if I don't know.'

Mrs Fishent: 'That makes sense.'

Mrs Praisall: 'And it goes right the way through the organisation, so that everyone is helping everyone else to do a better job.'

Mrs Fishent: 'Utopia!'

Mrs Praisall (laughing): 'Well, we just have to do the best we can!'

Mrs Fishent: 'Sounds more like the National Health!'

Mrs Praisall: 'First, I'd like to know more about all these things you're good at, because, as you say, I need to learn what goes on. Then I might have some ideas to help with one or two of the difficulties you've encountered, particularly handling problematic situations on the telephone. Also, I'll be most interested in those suggestions you've made about how the service can be improved overall, especially getting the whole team involved in the audits. Are you game to give it a try?'

Mrs Fishent: 'I'll try anything once!'

THINK BOX

How do *you* view appraisal?

Is it a purely benign process, designed to improve efficiency and happiness (in both individual and organisation)?

Is it a sinister institutional game of dominance?

Can you really trust anybody?

What is Mrs Praisall's agenda?

What is Mrs Fishent's agenda?

What is the Department of Health's agenda?

And who is pulling *their* tail?

What did you think of Mrs Praisall's negotiating skills?

How far do you think the 'mutually agreed plan' for Mrs Fishent will be a contract against which she is to be measured in another year's time?

Which of the following would you rather be, and why?

•   An appraiser.
•   An appraisee.

You can trust your health professional

Trust is the key issue in these challenging scenarios. The health professional establishes rapport, convinces you that they're on your side, and respects your individuality and your agenda. In a word, they defuse the situation. They use their communication skills in your service, and instead of confrontation, you're ready for negotiation. Well, that's the theory anyway (the *face* model again). The above examples may have shown you some of the ways in which it might work in practice. Can you really trust a manager, though?

Mad people have difficulty in organising their agendas. You can do it for them. Demanding and angry people may trigger your adrenaline pump, too. Focus on listening and use empathy to defuse the situation. Make sure that you have listened to the whole story of a complaint before commenting. Face-saving should usually be possible for both sides. Start from the recipient's level of understanding and their willingness to hear bad news. Chunk and check. Respond to their questions. Negotiation of the situation and roles is especially important during appraisal and when giving feedback. Emphasise the positive, be constructive, and avoid personal criticism if possible.

Respect for the other and willingness to help builds up trust.

The verbal and non-verbal skills required to deal with challenging situations are the same as those we have already encountered in Chapters 3 and 4. Use of these skills and the *face* model may result in your finding that fewer and fewer of these situations are as challenging as they used to be.

> Donald: 'He would say that, wouldn't he? I can't get on with all these dramatic scripts, and I'd like to put my fist through that face model of his.'
> Liam: 'Don't be such a grouch! I know he's a bit irritating, but getting the other person's agenda is only common sense, and doubly important in tricky situations.'
> Donald: 'I'm not convinced by the scripts. I'd need more detail to make them realistic. They're too short, and there's not enough about body language or silences.'
> Liam: 'Put it down to artistic licence. You've got to use a bit of imagination.'
> Donald: 'Anyway, I've thought of another "challenging situation" that he hasn't covered yet.'
> Liam: 'What's that?'
> Donald: 'It's when another person is present, and they keep interfering with the consultation.'
> Liam: 'You mean a relative?'
> Donald: 'Not always.'
> Liam: 'Well that's like a group, isn't it?'
> Donald: 'A group?'
> Liam: 'Yes, a group of three. Three agendas instead of two.'
> Donald: 'Oh no, not that model again!'

I'm afraid it is.

We shall deal with groups in Chapter 6.

CHAPTER SIX

Three (or more) needn't be a crowd
GROUPS

Donald: 'I hate groups.'

Liam: 'Why's that?'

Donald: 'They're full of noisy people. I get bored with listening to all the hot air. I can't get a word in edgeways, even if I want to.'

Liam: 'That's the leader's fault.'

Donald: 'Really? I've never found a group leader who seemed interested in my opinion, or even if I had one. Is that their job, then? Perhaps someone should tell them. Anyway, not all groups *have* leaders.'

Liam: 'Well, in that case maybe you need assertiveness training?'

Donald: 'That's just the kind of trendy thing you *would* suggest. I can make a noise if I want to, but I don't see why I should have to fire from the hip like some of them, spouting any kind of rubbish that comes into their heads, just to get noticed.'

Liam: 'Some people can't help it. They have to get all their thoughts out into the open, before they can work them out. I expect you do all that in your head, before you speak.'

Donald: 'I'm sure my thoughts are quite unlike the ridiculous things that I hear from some of them, but you're right – I *do* turn everything over and over in my mind. There's no point in speaking unless you have something worth listening to, in my opinion.'

Liam: 'It would be a silent world, indeed.'

Donald: 'Nothing wrong with silence. Anyway, by the time I've worked out my thoughts, they're already on to something else and I've lost interest.'

Liam: 'So you never take part?'

Donald: 'Very occasionally I get to say something, but everyone seems bored and can't wait for me to finish.'

Liam: 'That's a shame. Not *everything* you say is rubbish.'

Donald: '*Thanks!*'

THINK BOX

Is everything in a group down to the leader?

Should Donald be group leader instead of a member? He would then be expected to speak, but what if the group still ignored him and behaved as if there were no leader at all?

Do you have primary care team meetings?

Who leads, and how is that decided?

What is your role in the team, and is it fixed or does it change?

Is there anyone like Donald in your team and, if so, what do you do with them?

Trios

Hold everything. You might remember I've already said that three is a group (Eric Clapton on lead, Jack Bruce on bass and Ginger Baker on drums).

I'm showing my age again. The dynamics in *that* group were reputed to be complicated enough. Larger ones tend to get worse, but I believe that the principles are the same.

Perhaps the most common situation for the health professional is an interview or consultation in which a third party is present. Usually the third person is a relative, who may be there to amplify or emphasise parts of the story, or to make sure that some of it is not forgotten.

'Make sure you tell the doctor about the chest pains, Fred!'

'All right, dear.'

'I know you. I bet you'll come out not having said half of what you're supposed to. I'd better come with you!'

EXERCISE

Do you have a video of an interview where a third party was present? If not, you'll just have to look out the case-notes to remind you of what happened.

Why do you think the third person was there?

How do you know?

Did you try to involve the extra person, or did you try not to let them interfere with the main interview?

Why did you (or why didn't you) do this?

Was there any conflict?

If so, why, and between whom?

Who was 'in charge'?

How difficult do you find this type of encounter?

Why?

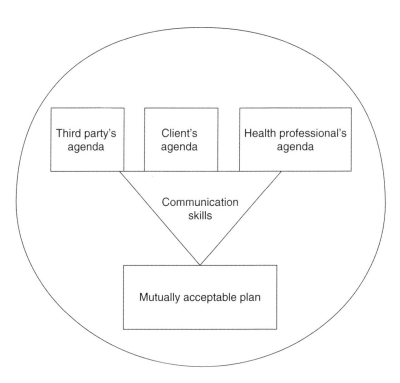

Figure 6.1

It's the *face* model with three eyes! There are three agendas, so it's 50% more complicated – potentially.

It is possible to ignore the third party completely, or it may be that they have just come along to keep their partner company. However, even third parties who are elsewhere can make their presence felt. Have you experienced this phenomenon?

'...only, I wish you'd check my blood pressure – otherwise the wife'll go on at me, and you know what she's like!'

It is often the case that the health professional is expected to be the leader of the group of three – for example, a consultation in a doctor's surgery is on the professional's territory. However, the expectations of role may not be so clear-cut when the encounter takes place at the client's own residence. Health visitors, nurses or doctors may become involved in an impromptu family conference.

'Before you go in there, we just want you to know that he mustn't be told the diagnosis.'

Even if the professional is granted the leadership role, it is necessary for them to take account of the wishes and feelings of all of the parties. Otherwise there is a strong likelihood of conflict.

> Dr Shorts: 'Come in and sit down, Fred. Have a seat, Mrs Bloggs. What can I do for you, Fred?'
>
> Fred: 'It's like this, doctor. I've not been feeling at all well lately.'
>
> Dr Shorts: 'Not at all well. In what way?'
>
> Fred: 'Well, tired, you know.'
>
> Dr Shorts: 'How tired?'
>
> Mrs Bloggs (sharply): 'You tell him about those pains in your chest, Fred!'
>
> Fred: 'I was coming to that...'
>
> Mrs Bloggs: 'He doesn't tell you half what's going on. He's had these pains going right down his arm into the fingers, and pins and needles something rotten!'
>
> Dr Shorts (without turning round): 'Fred, I need *you* to tell me in your own words.'
>
> Mrs Bloggs: 'He won't do that. Time and time again I've told him. Fred, I said, the doctor can't help you if he doesn't know what's going on!'
>
> Dr Shorts: 'Come on, Fred. You're the one with the pain. Only you can describe it.'
>
> Mrs Bloggs: 'It's sharp, like something tearing your heart out, isn't it Fred? He's never had a pain as bad as this, believe me doctor!'
>
> Dr Shorts (turning round, at last): 'I really do think Fred should speak for himself, Mrs Bloggs.'
>
> Mrs Bloggs: 'Do you now, doctor? My Fred's been coming here for weeks and weeks, and you still haven't found out what's wrong with him. I may not have passed exams like you, but I reckon I know a heart problem when it hits me in the eye. His old man was just the same, as you ought to know!'

> **THINK BOX**
>
> What should Dr Shorts do now?
>
> Have you ever been involved in a similar situation?
>
> If so, how did you cope with it?
>
> What do you think now about the exclusion of third parties?

'It wouldn't be so easy to shut me up, in a group of three,' says Donald.
'Thanks for the warning!,' says Liam.

Follow my leader

> **THINK BOX**
>
> I put it to you again. Does responsibility for the functioning of a group belong to the leader?
>
> Is Dr Shorts the leader, or is it now Mrs Bloggs?
>
> Does it really matter?
>
> What is the purpose of a leader anyway?

In my opinion, in a group of three, as in any other size of group, it is usually best to make sure that all of the agendas are addressed. Otherwise, the group may perform below its potential, or there may be trouble brewing. Any leader who ignores this risks losing influence over the group. It depends on the size of the group, how many are ignored, and how much power they are able to wield (quite a lot, in the case of Fred's wife).

Meanwhile, Dr Strait has convened a meeting of the primary healthcare team. You have already met some of the cast:

- Dr Shorts – the junior partner
- Dr Avenger – the clinical governance lead (you've heard of him anyway)
- Sister Brasstoff – practice nurse
- Sister O'Mercy – practice nurse
- Mrs Fishent – receptionist
- Mrs Chocbox – receptionist
- Mrs Praisall – the practice manager.

Here are some others that you haven't met:

- Nurse Practical – district nurse
- Sister Goodness – district nurse
- Ms Toe – the health visitor
- Mr Ladebak – the community psychiatric nurse (CPN)
- Mr Gruviman – the social worker
- Ms Statistic – a research officer from the clinical governance group.

Dr Strait: 'Welcome, everybody. I'm afraid the other doctors haven't yet returned from their calls, or are on their half days. It seems impossible to fix a day for this meeting that suits everyone. I'm especially glad to be able to welcome our CPN and social worker. I know you relate to more practices than just ours. Also, I'd like to welcome Ms Statistic. I'll leave Dr Avenger to introduce you more fully when he arrives.'

Ms Toe: 'Please can I put another item on the agenda? It's about cover for immunisation clinics and the inadequacy of my room. I did tell the secretary, but she's managed to miss it off.'

Dr Strait: 'You can have it under any other business, Linda.'

Ms Toe: 'I don't know if I can stay that long. I've another meeting at the health authority.'

Dr Strait: 'Well, perhaps we can get through the business fairly quickly. Let's see how we go for now.'

Nurse Practical (aside): 'You know Miss Phetid's ulcer?'

Sister Goodness: 'Oh yes, before I forget, have we doppler'd her? If not, we'd better talk to Dr Shorts about it.'

Dr Strait: 'Ahem!'

Sister Goodness: 'Sorry.'

Dr Strait: 'Very well. Can we crack on, everybody?' (He pauses.) 'As you know, or as some of you know, the main reason for this meeting is to see if we can work together as a team on a practice development plan, which we apparently need to do in order to satisfy the requirements of clinical governance. Ah, there you are, Rod! Since Dr Avenger has now appeared, I'll let him explain it in more detail.'

Dr Avenger: 'We're most fortunate to have Ms Statistic with us, as the first task for the primary care group is to carry out an audit of our diabetic care.'

Mrs Fishent: 'I hope you're going to involve the staff more than you did last time you tried an audit. Let's face it; that was a real fiasco!'

Dr Avenger: 'Well, I think we've learned some lessons and moved on from there.'

Nurse Practical (aside): 'I expect there'll still be plenty of dressings to do.'

Sister Goodness (aside): 'You can say that again. No matter how much reorganisation we have at the top, Miss Phetid's leg will still need doing.'

Nurse Practical (aside): 'And plenty of others besides.'

Dr Avenger (aside): 'I expect some of your leg ulcer patients are diabetic.'

Dr Strait: 'Can we stick to the topic? If you have something to say, please address the whole meeting.'

Dr Avenger: 'An audit of diabetic care will improve our care of diabetics, and will reduce complications like leg ulcers!'

Dr Strait: 'Sorry, Rod! I didn't mean you!'

Sister Brasstoff: 'It's about time we updated our diabetic protocol, anyway. Now we've got HbA_{1c} instead of HbA_1, nobody will tell me what is an acceptable result, as opposed to a desirable one.'

Mr Gruviman: 'You've lost me with all this technical stuff. I just came to re-establish contact, so if you've no specific problems in my field...'

Dr Avenger: 'I'm sure our diabetic patients have more than their share of social problems.'

Mr Gruviman: 'Yeah, well, when you've worked out who they are and what problems they have, perhaps you'll be in contact – only it probably won't be me who takes the message. There's a duty officer, as you probably know.' (He leaves.)

Mr Ladebak: 'I'm in a similar sort of position, you know. My role has changed a bit since we last met. It's all due to "care in the community", I'm afraid. A lot of people are going off sick with stress because of it. Now, if you were planning to audit the care of the chronic mentally sick, I might be able to do business with you. I don't suppose you want to volunteer to be key workers for any of the patients on your list?'

Dr Avenger: 'We've been into all that at the LMC.'

Mr Ladebak: 'Yes, I know. See you around.'

Dr Strait: 'Thanks for coming, anyway.'

Dr Avenger: 'Without further ado, I'd like to introduce Ms Statistic from the CG unit. She's going to tell us about the audit in more detail. Lee Ding, the floor is yours!'

Ms Toe: 'I'm sorry to butt in, but I'm feeling more and more angry!'

Dr Strait: 'Why is that, Linda?'

Ms Toe: 'Don't patronise me, Dr Strait! You call this a primary care team meeting? I've never seen such a shambles in all my life!'

Dr Strait: 'What do you mean?'

Ms Toe: 'There's no leadership in this practice! Half the people here have no interest in your precious diabetic audit, and all the nurses have already got personal development plans. If you'd find out beforehand what the members of your team want, you'd have more chance of running an effective meeting. In the meantime, I'm having to use part of the corridor for child health surveillance because, as you well know, my room is far too small!'

Dr Strait: 'Well, the issue of premises is far from simple, since the advent of the PCG. We might be able to swap rooms round if you could be more flexible about the time of day for these clinics.'

Dr Avenger: 'I'm sorry about this, Lee Ding. I thought the agenda had been circulated well before the meeting.'

Ms Statistic: 'That's another lunch you owe me, 007!'

Dr Avenger: 'The pleasure's all mine, Moneypenny!'

THINK BOX

Who do you think was the leader in the above primary care team meeting?

Why do you think this?

Did the leader have a mandate?

Is it obvious who should lead the team (in general)?

Why or why not?

How would you rate the performance of the leader here?

Lippitt and White investigated three leadership styles:

- authoritarian
- democratic
- *laissez-faire*.

The authoritarian leader gave strong direction, the democratic leader facilitated the group to find its own direction, and the *laissez-faire* leader was virtually uninvolved.

One of the three groups showed more interest, did better quality work and was more efficient at problem-solving. (As Clive James would say – which one? I'll ask the lovely Samantha (or Sven) to open the envelope with the winner's name inside – listeners on radio will just have to use their imaginations.) And the winner is:

The democratic group!

Not only did the authoritarian-led group lose, but they also exhibited an excess of aggressive behaviour in the process.

How did the democrats do it? Well, according to Maier,[1] the quality of thinking in a democracy depends on the ability of minority opinions to be heard. What does that mean? I'm sorry to keep saying this (well, no, I'm not sorry actually), but it's *agendas* again, isn't it?

'He's saying that they should listen to *my* opinion,' says Donald.

'I thought you couldn't stand the *face* model,' says Liam.

THINK BOX

How do people become leaders in a group?

How did it happen in your groups?

What kind of people are the leaders?

Can other types of people make good leaders?

What do leaders actually do?

Some leaders are appointed (i.e. imposed from outside the group). This kind of leader may have a commitment to push the group to meet the objectives of a larger organisation, thus tending towards a more authoritarian style. Groups may elect their own leaders (by more or less democratic means). These may be people with recognised expertise, good problem-solving skills, perceived importance or mere popularity. Leaders may emerge without being formally elected, during the group process. Sometimes the person who seizes the initiative, by being the first to speak (particularly if the task appears to be difficult), becomes the leader. Leadership is not necessarily fixed (even for the duration of a single meeting), particularly if there has been no formal appointment or election. Movement of the leadership role depends on the composition of the group and the task in hand.

It makes sense, therefore, that a great variety of personality types can be successful leaders in appropriate circumstances. War leaders are often less effective in peacetime. Nevertheless, it seems that 'natural' leaders are more often extrovert, confident, sociable and relaxed. They may be nice guys, but are they any good as leaders? Should the President be a movie star, with the real decisions being made by figures in the background? Is your leader the puppet of an organisation?

'I've always distrusted leaders,' says Donald. 'Why not just do away with them?'
'Off with their heads!,' says Liam. 'Anyway, there are groups without leaders.'
'I bet they work just fine,' says Donald.
'Actually they can,' says Liam. 'It depends on the group, though.'
'What do leaders *do*?,' says Donald. 'What use are they, especially if they won't allow me to speak?'

John Heron described the following six categories of intervention that could be made by a group leader.[2]

1   Prescribe (an action or a topic).
2   Inform (summarise, interrelate, clarify knowledge).
3   Confront (challenge, disagree, criticise).
4   Release tension (catharsis).

5   Elicit (draw out, facilitate, catalyse).
6   Support (approve, reinforce).

He also described the following methods of facilitation:

*   scanning the group (see who wants to speak)
*   'traffic cop' (hand signals to stop or start contributions)
*   eye contact
*   head gestures and position
*   open questions
*   closed questions
*   reflection (echo the last few words)
*   selective reflection (echo part of what was said)
*   check for understanding
*   emphasising.

(I've seen an orchestra, as well as a group, conducted by eyebrow movements – but back to John Heron.)

He described the following comments on the 'process' (what was going on in the group):

*   attributive (of a psychological state, e.g. 'you are angry')
*   psychodynamic (referring to a theory, e.g. transactional analysis)
*   sociodynamic (group dynamics, e.g. contribution rates, social roles, dominance, dependence, reaction to the leader)
*   transpersonal comments (something outside normal experience).

'Sounds a bit far out, man!,' says Liam.

'Emperor's new clothes, that last one,' says Donald. 'The others sound really sensible, though – but am I going crazy? Perhaps I'm just a bit dense, but I've never *seen* leaders doing things like that.'

'I didn't say a word!,' says Liam.

Many of the interventions and skills described by John Heron are also applicable to the one-to-one situation (*see* Chapters 3 and 4). For example, there are strong similarities with the counselling model. There's quite a lot to it, though, isn't there? Perhaps leaders should have more training?

THINK BOX

Is group leadership more difficult than communication with one person?

If so, why (or if not, why not)?

What would you say is the main problem for a group leader?

In general terms, how would you attempt to overcome it?

How can some groups be successful without a leader?

I don't know if you've ever experienced *leaderless groups*, still less those that actually work? In my experience, most of them are relatively ineffective and sometimes disastrous. The worst scenario seems to occur when members of a group actively reject the leadership role, perhaps because members have problems with status, or because they feel themselves to be past the 'adolescent' stage of needing structure and rules. Such groups are often saved by the emergence of leadership by one or more members, whether or not this is acknowledged by the others.

In order to work well, groups need to benefit from the functions of leadership (which have been well set out by John Heron).[2] This can happen without a leader in the accepted sense. The secret is that *the group does it for itself*, almost as though it were some kind of organism made up of interdependent parts that work in harmony. You might say, on close observation, that the leadership function passes smoothly and seamlessly between different members of the group according to the task in hand and the talents or expertise of the individuals.

This is most likely to happen with a small group of individuals who know each others' roles and skills extremely well, and who have a high degree of trust of one another. Occasionally, it might happen with a group of relative strangers who just 'click'. However, 'total football' is the product of intensive training, despite its natural appearance. Personally, I feel happier if the goalkeeper in the team I support stays in his own half of the field!

When the 'process' gets in the way

Sometimes running groups can feel like trying to herd cats. There's too much independence, and too much scrapping over territory. Does this remind you of the primary care team? It would be easier if all the problems were immediately apparent, but this is rarely the case.

There are undercurrents!

Sigmund Freud became involved with these, as you might imagine. He found groups to be characterised by an increase in emotional forces, at the expense of intellectual functioning.[3] He blamed libidinal forces which caused feelings of ambivalence towards the leader. I'm sure you can hardly wait to read about all this, so off you go to the bibliography. I think I'll just take a cold shower, if you don't mind.

Perhaps we can agree that *there are conflicting forces, some of which are unconscious.* Bion talked about the *conflict between individual needs and group mentality/culture.*[4] He stated that, *within every group, there is a work group and a basic assumption group.* The latter function deals with anxiety (fight or flight), complacency (dependency) and guilt (pairing behaviour). A more recent term for this is *process.*

Once upon a time, before he knew better, Dr Shorts joined a GP trainers' 'process group', although he had no idea what that meant. There was a choice between that and a 'task group', which sounded as if it might be boring. Dr Shorts was very anxious to find out what a 'process group' might be all about. Off he went to the first meeting and, to his great astonishment, nobody spoke. This was very frustrating, as he wanted to learn how to become a trainer, and no one would tell him. He had left a good book at home that evening, otherwise he would have seriously considered getting it out. Why didn't he either ask someone what was going on, or just walk out? Well, he sensed that speaking might be the wrong thing to do and, to be honest, he was more than a little curious. Fortunately, for him, someone else decided to speak. He didn't know if they had a very low tolerance for silence or whether there was some other reason.

'Nice day.'

'*Nice?*'

'Yes, nice.'

'That's avoiding the issue.'

'The issue?'

'You know.'

This enigmatic little exchange was again followed by silence. Afterwards, there were sporadic contributions by other members of the group, often accompanied by minute analysis of the possible meanings of each word uttered in response. It was not clear who, if anyone, was leader, and neither Dr Shorts nor any of the other newcomers, was acknowledged. Equally, it seemed impossible to recognise a possible entry point, so as to be able to make a contribution. Eventually, another member, who had sat with his head down during the entire proceedings, jerked upright.

'Every time you open your mouth,' he said, fixing a venomous stare at the opposite side of the circle, 'I want to punch it really hard!'

Exciting, don't you think? There were certainly conflicting forces, and there were *hidden agendas* (at least to me they were hidden). Later I came to understand that 'process groups' are supposed to deal with (and learn from) the group dynamics.

THINK BOX

Look back at the dialogue from Dr Strait's team meeting.

How many different things were going wrong in that meeting?

What was the leadership style?

What interventions or skills from the John Heron armoury were employed?

What others might have helped, had they been employed?

In a group of eight people, there are only eight different agendas but 28 possible relationships going on. It becomes increasingly difficult to work with larger groups than this, because the dynamics increase exponentially, and because a large audience is inhibiting to most people.

Michael and Maggie Kindred have provided a catalogue of possible difficulties, accompanied by amusing cartoons (for more details, you should read the booklet):[5]

- members not clear about the purpose of the group
- unsuitable room and facilities, seating arrangements and timing
- intrusive refreshment breaks
- names and titles not negotiated
- variable membership
- confidentiality issues
- interruptions
- personal and topic boundaries not defined
- smoking
- task versus process
- feeling excluded
- bids for control
- interpersonal feelings
- anxiety
- extroverts and introverts
- non-verbal cues ignored
- opting out
- lack of sensitivity to others' feelings
- not listening (not only to what is said)
- dominance behaviour
- authoritarian leadership
- conflict with co-leader
- sub-groups
- pairing

- red herrings
- over-involvement
- subversive behaviour
- indecision
- confusion about group rules
- emotional barriers
- hidden agendas
- projection on to others
- scapegoating
- the group 'casualty'
- stereotyping
- point scoring
- hobby horses
- over-dependence on the leader
- unplanned silences
- sexuality
- major issue left until the end.

THINK BOX

Has the above list helped you to identify any more problems in Dr Strait's team meeting?

Bolden and colleagues advised group leaders (in general practice vocational training) to focus on the feelings of individuals (particularly through non-verbal behaviour), rather than on the feel of the group as a whole.[6] They noticed a tendency for men to interrupt women, a lack of sensitivity to quiet members, and relentless questioning of individuals by the rest of the group. There was also a phenomenon which they called 'uproar', where an extrovert member who was confronted with creating a diversion would question the competence of the leader (something similar occurred in Dr Strait's meeting, didn't it?).

Sorry, I'm on a role

To understand what happens in groups, we have to get to grips with the variety of possible roles that can be played by members. So far we have only considered the role of leader. Before we look at other roles that can be played within the group, let us turn our attention to those roles which people already have outside the group.

THINK BOX

Turning back to Dr Strait's team meeting, how many outside roles could you identify?

Of course, the main roles are connected with the different jobs that people do. For example, Ms Toe is a health visitor. However, people do have other roles, such as parent (in the case of Dr Strait) or clinical governance leader as well as GP and perhaps 'Don Juan' (in the case of Dr Avenger).

THINK BOX

Write a concise description of the jobs of all the other types of primary healthcare professional apart from your own.

Ask the others to write a description of yours.

Now compare notes and write down the main differences in perception.

To help me with some of the background for this book, I had discussions with our own district nurses (who without exception are wonderful). When I asked about their perception of the doctor's job, they said that it was more technical and that we tended to ignore feelings. Well, I suppose I did ask for it! How many surprises did you get?

Misunderstanding of each others' roles is an important barrier to multidisciplinary team work.

These perceptions form an important part of our *agendas* in relation to other members of the team. However, within the team, there are other roles which are dependent on our different personalities. Belbin has produced a questionnaire to identify the following nine types that seem to be important in teams.[7]

1 Completer–finisher:
   - great capacity for follow-through and attention to detail
   - unlikely to start a task they cannot finish
   - typically anxious and introverted
   - poor tolerance of 'casual' colleagues
   - poor delegator
   - good at concentration, accuracy, achieving high standards and meeting deadlines.
2 Implementor:
   - practical, systematic and disciplined
   - loyal hard worker
   - tendency to rigidity
   - reliable, efficient and knows what needs to be done.
3 Monitor–evaluator:
   - serious-minded and cautious
   - thinks slowly and critically about all factors
   - good judgement skills
   - able to analyse problems, ideas and options.

4   Specialist:
 •   single-minded with high professional standards
 •   expert in a narrow field, but lacking interest in others
 •   decisions based on in-depth knowledge and experience
5   Co-ordinator:
 •   able to persuade others to work towards shared goals
 •   mature, broad-minded, trusting, confident and respected
 •   good delegator
 •   good at spotting and using talent for group objectives
 •   calm leadership style that is effective with peers
 •   style may clash with 'shapers'.
6   Team worker:
 •   mild, sociable, supportive and concerned about others
 •   very supportive of the team
 •   flexible, adaptable, sensitive, perceptive and diplomatic
 •   good listener
 •   popular
 •   can be indecisive
 •   good at raising morale, reducing conflict and promoting co-operation.
7   Resource investigator:
 •   enthusiastic, extrovert, relaxed and inquisitive
 •   good negotiator and communicator
 •   can think on their feet
 •   good developer of others' ideas, investigator of contacts and resources
 •   needs constant stimulation of others.
8   Shaper:
 •   aggressive, single-minded, competitive, extrovert with strong drive
 •   challenge to win, argumentative
 •   pushy leadership style, thrives under pressure
 •   good at overcoming obstacles, otherwise frustration results
 •   may lack understanding of others, prepared to take unpopular decisions
 •   good at achieving positive action.
9   Plant:
 •   creative innovator
 •   introvert, unorthodox and impractical
 •   poor communicator
 •   sensitive to praise or criticism
 •   good at generating new ideas and solving complex problems.

'I've identified which one you are, Donald,' says Liam.

'Which one?,' says Donald.

'The evaluator, of course,' says Liam, 'and I'm a plant.'

'Pass me the weed-killer,' says Donald.

EXERCISE

Where would you place yourself in the Belbin classification?

Write notes on the characteristics of the people in your team(s)

Which Belbin types are present in your teams?

Are there any types missing?

Does it matter?

Why?

Perhaps you found it difficult to assign yourself or your colleagues to one definite Belbin type. Most people tend to be mixtures of these categories, which means that they are able to play more than one role in a group, if the situation calls for it.

Some groups are dysfunctional because they have an adverse composition. For example, lack of a completer–finisher can be a problem. The presence of too many shapers and/or too many plants is associated with conflict, as they may all be pulling in different directions.

A life in the days of a group

'Storming, norming...something like that,' says Liam.

'You're not thinking of the Gulf war?,' says Donald.

'You mean "Stormin' Norman",' says Liam.

'That's right,' says Donald. 'Perhaps you were referring to toothbrushes?'

'What?' says Liam.

'Norman Wisdom,' says Donald.

'I think I preferred you as an evaluator,' says Liam.

THINK BOX

Consider the group(s) of which you have been a member.

How have they changed, if at all, over time?

What was it like at the beginning?

What was it like near the end?

If you have been in groups on residential courses, how would you compare their evolution (in terms of speed and outcome) with that of other groups?

A developmental model for groups (after Tuckman) is described in the book by Patrick McEvoy.[8]

1 *Forming* – defining the nature and boundaries of the task:
   • grumbling about the task or setting
   • a meandering, ineffective approach to the task
   • suspicion of the task and each other
   • testing the leader and each other
   • hesitation or avoidance behaviour in relation to the task.
2 *Storming* – questioning the value of the exercise:
   • challenging the leader and each other
   • experimenting with hostility, aggression and frustration
   • defensively resisting self-disclosure
   • showing rivalry, argument, rebellion and opposition.
3 *Norming* – opening up and inviting each other to:
   • express feelings
   • redefine the task
   • give and take opinions, and evaluate them
   • feel like a group
   • offer mutual support and build special relationships
   • clarify leadership and show more unity and consensus
   • show more cohesion and group feeling, and less interest in extrinsic factors.
4 *Performing* – pursuing the task effectively by:
   • contributing frequently and mutually
   • showing more insight and understanding of the task
   • not worrying about interpersonal issues (which have already been sorted out or relegated)
   • feeling safe and confident about the identity and task of the group
   • gaining real achievements.
5 *Ending* – facing the loss of the group experience:
   • by denial (we'll meet again)
   • by bargaining (task not yet complete)
   • with anger (nobody appreciates us)
   • with depression
   • with a sense of ritual.

THINK BOX

Do you recognise your own groups in the above developmental model?

What stage are you at now?

How do you know?

Does it help to know where you are?

At what stage is Dr Strait's team?

Would it help him to know?

As a fledgeling group leader, I would certainly have found it helpful to have had this model available as a rough chart to help me navigate choppy waters. It is all too easy to take what appears to be negative behaviour personally, instead of being able to see it for what it really is, namely a necessary part of group development. Many group leaders must have felt that they were failures at the 'storming' stage, in particular.

Awareness of group process is also an asset to any other member, not just the leader. This can be used to assist the leader in the task of facilitation, or to accept the baton for a while, if appropriate. In a group of sophisticates, the leadership issue may become less important as each member lends a hand. Alternatively, those who are experts at 'playing the game' may indulge in complex power struggles. One of these games is 'we don't need rules or leaders because we're grown-ups'. The consequent dysfunction becomes an end in itself. I suspect that the 'process group' that I stumbled into all those years ago was one of this type.

Self-doubt is a problem for leaders and members alike. If the latter feel that the group is out of control, and that the leader has no idea what to do, panic may well set in. On the other hand, a relaxed approach in the face of difficulties helps the group to feel the same. As the man on stilts at the village fête said: *'Don't panic – at least I know what I'm doing!'*

An experienced leader learns to give the group room to breathe, to make mistakes and to feel uncomfortable as a result. Allowing the group to have ownership of its own problems, by reflecting perceptions back, leads to *solutions by the group*.

'I bet he wears sandals,' says Donald.
'With socks,' says Liam.

Intellectual punch-ups

Buck Mulligan (in James Joyce's *Ulysses*) claimed expertise in this field.

Democratic group leaders are the top managers in this particular variety of sport. Unfortunately, group work can turn into a blood sport and healthy debate can degenerate into a series of gladiatorial encounters. Extroverts take part with relish, but introverts usually withdraw from such conflict.

Seen on a tablet in ancient Rome: SHOCK RESULT! CHRISTIANS BEAT LIONS!

There is also a phenomenon known as the *risky shift*, which can occur in group decision-making. It appears that some individuals can be persuaded to choose riskier options when bolstered by a group than they would choose alone. Sometimes this can be explained by the pressure of a vociferous majority on one or two deviates or isolates in the group who may then agree to support action which they know in their hearts to be incorrect. There is a strong resemblance here to George Orwell's 'double think'. The pressure to make questionable decisions is likely to be more intense when a course of action is pushed by an influential, exciting and charismatic leader with an axe to grind. Sieg Heil!

Janis highlighted problems connected with *group think*:[8]

• discussion of a limited range of options
• failure to re-examine initially preferred options
• failure to re-examine other options
• failure to make use of expert opinion
• selective bias in evaluating expert opinion
• limited discussion of possible drawbacks of proposed action.

The overall effect of 'group think' is inadequate evaluation of a constricted range of options. Paradoxically, the strength of a group, as opposed to an individual, ought to be *the range of options and insights available for consideration*. Perhaps the operative word in the last sentence is 'available'. Some groups simply do not use their own strengths, because they fail to allow the airing and exploration of individual *agendas*.

'Dead right!' says Donald.
'But It's the *face* model again,' says Liam.
'Maybe there's something in it, after all,' says Donald.

THINK BOX

Have you ever been persuaded of something, against your better judgement, by a powerful majority?

To what extent does 'group think' affect your groups?

How would you change the way your groups are run, in order to try to minimise the problems of 'group think'?

Janis suggested that 'group think' could be counteracted by the following:
• encouraging 'devil's advocacy' and conflicts
• giving priority to doubts and uncertainties
• the leader tolerating criticism of his or her judgement
• avoiding preferred courses of action in the 'brief'.

Lewin suggested that the development of group *norms* is dependent on decisions being made on the initiative of the group, and not forced by the leader.[10] In this situation, discussion can lead to creative (and sometimes unexpected) decisions. The whole process depends on the *encouragement of a diversity of views*.

Hall and Watson talked about *the institutionalisation of conflict, and the crucial role of the leader in fostering this*.[11] The elements of the process appear to consist of the following:

- discussion
- confrontation
- plurality of choices
- consensual decision-making.

Group members, including the introverts (some of whom may be experts), need a safe environment in which to share their agendas with the others. They need to be confident that their individuality and their views will be *respected*, that debate will be constructive, and that the result is not a foregone conclusion. It is the responsibility of all group members, particularly those with superior social skills, to support these aims. Democratic leadership, sensitive to the needs of individuals, is a vital component of this process. Indeed, the *face* model strikes again!

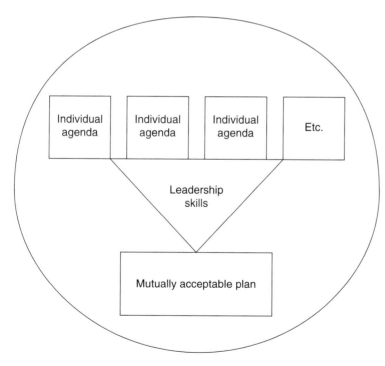

Figure 6.2

In a group of three, the health professional must attend to the agenda of the third party as well as that of the client. As there are often constraints which make it more difficult to connect with this third agenda, the professional must be particularly careful to attend to the non-verbal cues of the mute bystander. In groups, the constraints on individual expression are often greatly increased, and sensitivity to non-verbal behaviour is therefore of paramount importance. The skills are the same as those described in Chapters 3 and 4, but the arena is larger. At times, the group leader must have eyes in the back of his or her head.

Nevertheless, I repeat my view that the responsibility is a shared one. After all, the group's problems belong to the group. A skilled leader can draw those problems to the group's attention largely by attending to non-verbal cues. It is also particularly helpful if the leader helps the group to define boundaries and rules at the beginning, which help the members to feel confident about sharing their agendas. These provide the plurality of options necessary for high-quality decision-making.

Now rewind the video. Enter Dr Strait and the team.

Dr Strait: 'I know it's very difficult to get everyone together at once, but thank you all for making the effort. I think we have enough representatives of the different groups here, so that we can all go back and liaise with the others' (he looks round to gauge the level of attention and agreement). 'As you will all know, the primary care group requires us to produce a practice development plan. However, the details are very much up to us, and I thought that it would be an opportunity to work together as a team. Also, the PCG has specified an audit of diabetic care to be done throughout the group, and I would like as wide an involvement of team members as possible, to ensure a good result' (he pauses and looks round again). 'The main thing, though, is to hear the views of everybody on how we can work more closely together as a team. We need to listen to these views and respect them. That would be a valuable start. Any questions, at this stage?'

Ms Toe: 'What about the facilities for the child health surveillance clinics? My room is far too small for the purpose.'

Dr Strait: 'I agree that it's unsatisfactory. We need to look at the possible options in detail. It would be helpful if you could prepare some suggestions, and then perhaps I could meet with you separately?'

Ms Toe: 'All right, I'll get my diary after the meeting.'

Dr Strait: 'Fine, but that's a detail. The problem for me is that I don't really understand what some other members of the team do, and what their main problems are. It might be a start to give everyone a chance to say something about themselves and the job that they do' (he glances round). 'Sister Brasstoff, you're looking a bit puzzled.'

Sister Brasstoff: 'Well, you doctors know what we do, because you've written all the protocols.'

Dr Strait: 'That's true, but you have expressed a wish to develop the practice nurse's role, and your views about the patients' needs are based on a lot of experience. I'd also like to hear from the district nurses, who usually keep pretty quiet. I think you already have some experience of personal development plans and portfolios?'

Nurse Practical: 'Yes, but I thought you were talking about a practice development plan.'

Dr Avenger: 'It's important that we integrate our personal learning needs with the practice plan. It will be interesting to find out areas of need that we have in common.'

At this point, the videotape disintegrates!

I can't keep this up for ever. At least they're talking.

Quality assurance

Clinical governance, which should now be built into healthcare at all levels, has a strong resemblance to the concept of *total quality management* (TQM), which originated in the Japanese manufacturing industry. The aim of TQM is to increase profits by constantly improving the product in relation to the customer's needs. The main problem with the process, as applied to the National Health Service, is the absence of profits. Indeed, there are strong pressures against desirable investment, as it is funded by taxation.

In private industry, greater profits are available to fund investment for further quality improvement. Thus there is an incentive to help the workers to do their jobs more effectively, and to reward them for this. In the public sector, poor investment may mean increased demands on the workers, combined with relative lack of support or reward. There is a consequent danger that quality improvement may be hampered by apathy and burnout among the health workers.

In industry, specific areas of the process are the focus of *quality circles,* which are small teams of people working towards common aims. To some extent, these resemble practice teams working on their development plans. At the individual level, personal learning plans and appraisal are equally relevant in industry and in healthcare. The common objective of all of these is continually to drive up quality.

So look after the members of your team. Respect them, listen to their ideas, reward them and help them to do a better job. This is true for TQM and it is also true for all of the groups we have been considering.

As for learning needs, those are agendas as well. Chapter 7 is about the use of the *face* model in learning and teaching.

CHAPTER SEVEN

Tell me what I need and I'll tell you what I want
TEACHING AND LEARNING

> Donald: 'I've got this sickening feeling I know what's coming next.'
> Liam: 'Learner's agenda?'
> Donald: 'Teacher's agenda.'
> Liam: 'Put them both together...'
> Donald: 'And they all live happily ever after.'

Sarcasm is the lowest form of wit. Anyway, I think they're beginning to sound a bit like Tweedledum and Tweedledee. Just ignore them and they might go away. Now, where was I?

Where do you start?

Once upon a time, there was a keen young doctor called Shorts, who became a trainer of GPs. He'd been to all the courses, played 'ring-a-ring-a-roses' and make-believe. The practice was up to scratch, and he'd been video'd to death and interviewed. The teaching time was well protected and the receptionists were briefed. The next week, his first GP registrar was due to arrive.

HELP!

What do I do? All of those tutorial slots to be filled! What if I run out of things to talk about? What if I run out of things to say? What if he knows more than I do?

Pull yourself together, man! Go back to your course notes. What's the first thing they say?

Start from where the learner is.

'But where *is* the learner?', says Dr Shorts.

'On holiday', says Donald, 'but next week he'll be in your surgery!'.

Excuse me one moment (sounds of someone being strangled off-stage). Sorry about that. Now can I mention the word *agenda*?

What does the learner want from you? That's his agenda, isn't it? To learn how to write macho prescriptions for clot-busters? To bark out orders to the patients and the rest of the team? To be barked at by Sister Brasstoff?

Those are all guesses, of course, and perhaps not particularly good guesses. How will you find out?

'Ask him,' says Dr Shorts.

THINK BOX

Do you ask learners what they want?

If so, how do you do it?

What problems have you had with this?

If you don't ask, do you sometimes wish you had?

Why?

Do learners have anything else on their agendas, apart from wants?

'Their interests, where they've come from and their own self-assessment,' says Dr Shorts.
    What's that?

'Their agenda,' says Dr Shorts. 'All of those things are connected with the *wants* that they have and, I suppose, their *needs* as well.'

I'll come back to needs. Anything else?

'Where they want to go – I mean their career intentions, and how they think they might have to get there. Those are on their *agenda* as well,' says Dr Shorts.

Excuse me while I put up an overhead.

Learner's agenda

This consists of the following:

- goals
- previous experiences and interests
- self-assessment of attributes and abilities
- preferred methods
- ideas and reasoning.

Dr Shorts might assume that his new registrar wants to become a GP, just like him. However, this is by no means a foregone conclusion. In any case, how much will the job itself have changed in the next five years? Will the new doctor live and breathe medicine (and is that such a good thing?) or will he be more interested in watching football instead of reading in his spare time? What kind of person will Dr Shorts have to teach? How well will he know himself, his strengths and weaknesses? How does he prefer to learn? What makes him think the way he does? Human beings have complicated agendas. Perhaps just asking what he wants will be nowhere near adequate.

What's on *your* agenda, Dr Shorts?

'Well, first I have to discover his wants, of course – and all the rest of his agenda. Then I have to find out his real needs.'

Who are *you* to say what they are?

'Don't say that! I've already developed enough insecurity about my role as it is. Anyway, it's my job. I'm the teacher!'

Sorry. Of course you are. All I meant was that a person might be very good at assessing their own needs, and what you think they need might be more to do with what you want to teach.

'Oh dear! It's getting very complicated. Still, I can see your point about teaching preferences. Obviously, I'd much prefer to teach something I'm good at, but then, perhaps, they'd need something that I know nothing about. That's one of my worst fears, as a teacher.'

THINK BOX

How do you tell the difference between wants and needs in education?

Who is most likely to know about real needs?

- The individual.

- The organisation.

- The profession.

- The state.

- The clients.

'I'm tired of all this philosophy,' says Donald. 'It's quite simple. Wants are what people think they need. Needs are what you can measure. Truth instead of self-deception!'

'Ah, but what is truth?,' says Liam.

'Don't come the Pontius Pilate with me!,' says Donald. 'Anyway, what has all this to do with communication?'

'Agendas,' says Liam. 'Explore the agendas before negotiating a plan.'

'Doh!,' says Donald.

What else is on *your* agenda, Dr Shorts?

'Well, apart from finding out their wants and what I think they need, there are goals of teaching, aren't there? I mean there has to be some idea of an end product. That will also determine what their needs are.'

Where do the goals come from?

'Well, I guess most of it is laid down, isn't it? To some extent, it's led by the profession, but I suppose they're heavily influenced by the government. After all, that's where the funds come from.'

What about yourself?

'Me?'

Yes, you. Don't tell me that you have no ideas about the goals of teaching.'

'I do have ideas.'

Where do they come from, those ideas?

'Yes, of course. I do see that they're connected with my own personality and history. It's just the same as agendas in the consultation, isn't it?'

This calls for another overhead, I think!

Teacher's agenda

This consists of the following:

- assessment of learner's wants and goals
- assessment of learner's needs
- goals (individual, organisational and national)
- previous experiences and interests
- preferred methods
- ideas and reasoning.

THINK BOX

Philosophy apart, in practical terms, do you think that 'needs' are what the teacher identifies and 'wants' are what the learner has?

To what extent is this the case?

Would you say that one of the main tasks of a teacher is to convert 'needs' into 'wants'?

How would you do that?

'This is all very long-winded,' says Donald. 'I thought communication in relation to teaching and learning would be about presentation skills, in the main.'

'You can go and give your highly polished lecture, but it might be to an empty theatre!,' says Liam.

'You'd be surprised!,' says Donald. 'Some people love lectures.'

Investigating Rita

'Meet your new registrar, Dr Snow–Whyte,' says Mrs Praisall.

'Pleased to meet you. My name's Rita.'

'Help!,' thinks Dr Shorts. 'How am I going to explain this to my wife? I could have sworn that the course organiser said Dr Whyte was male!'

'I expect you'll be looking forward to all those one-to-one tutorials,' hisses Sister Brasstoff, aside.

We'll leave Dr Shorts to his panic for the moment. Of course, none of *us* would have allowed that situation to occur, would we? I mean – the very thought of a learner just turning up on the first day, without having had a meeting or without having found anything out about them. Not to mention all those assumptions about gender, watching football and the like. Serves him right, I say.

Start from where the learner is – needs and wants. You need as much information as you can get, if you want the teaching to be on target. Some things are easy to be sure about, or else you can measure them objectively. However, others are more subjective, especially when all you have to go on is what they tell you.

THINK BOX

What kinds of subjective information can you gather about needs or wants?

What objective methods are available?

Which of the two types interests you most?

Why?

Understanding another human being is impossible according to Jean-Paul Sartre.[1] At any rate, you'll probably agree that people are incredibly complex and often full of contradictions. Social scientists try to overcome this by using the approach of *multiple perspectives* – that is, coming at the problem from different angles. Health professionals might argue that the important thing is *performance* in the field of work, whatever goes on inside the individual's head. Some would add the proviso that the most important things are not necessarily the easiest ones to measure.

Multiple perspectives are useful for the teacher, too. Here are some ideas for Rita's initial assessment.

Assessment

This could include the following:

*   review of curriculum vitae and references
*   interview
*   self-report (using a check-list of desired competences)
*   multiple-choice questions
*   questions on case scenarios
*   attitude questionnaire
*   learning style questionnaire
*   observed interviews with clients (video or sitting in).

This is a menu from which to choose, rather than a compulsory battery of investigations to be performed at once! Nevertheless, there are other sources of information which could be used, such as review of referrals and investigations, and feedback from other members of staff, especially as the term proceeds. Poor Rita!

I mean it. Assessment is very important, but Rita needs to understand what is happening and why. She also has to agree to it. The two things go together – consent and understanding, that is. As always, good communication is essential. Rita wants to know *what the teacher's agenda is*. What is all this assessment for? Will there be a secret file? Who will be allowed to see it? There's something here about *respect* for the individual, and *trust*. You cannot evade these issues in communication.

My brother or my keeper?

What role does Dr Shorts have in relation to Dr Snow–Whyte? It might be any of the following:

*   teacher
*   fellow learner
*   mentor
*   elder brother figure
*   friend
*   employer
*   summative assessor
*   referee
*   doctor (probably inadvisable).

All of these roles are possible, but to what extent are they compatible with one another?
Rest assured, his wife will be interested in his reply to this question.

THINK BOX

What roles do you fulfil as a teacher?

What roles do you fulfil/have you fulfilled as a learner in primary healthcare?

What conflicts have you experienced in these roles?

How did you resolve them?

A meeting of minds

A teacher–learner relationship based on trust is best achieved by honest sharing of agendas. The possible conflicts of interest are best brought out into the open for discussion. In particular, whilst the learner is being exhorted to expose areas of deficiency for the purpose of formative development, those very deficiencies have the potential to be used as evidence to submit to higher authorities by the teacher. To what extent is the teacher a *double agent*?

THINK BOX

Do you ever view yourself, in the role of a teacher, as being a 'double agent'?

Under what circumstances would you be prepared to go to a higher authority to express your concerns about a learner?

Are you aware of a mechanism for this to occur?

How would you explain this potential situation to a learner?

As a learner, how might you feel about it?

It is usually much easier to come to an understanding about such issues in advance (and we shall return to this in relation to contracts). The question of divided loyalties is difficult. As a health worker, my first duty is to the patient, in terms of both their immediate healthcare needs and the quality of the health professionals that I help to train. These considerations should supersede any personal loyalties. Therefore, if I consider that a patient or client is at risk because of the actions of a learner, it is my duty to see that those actions are put right.

THINK BOX

In a debriefing session with Dr Snow–Whyte, Dr Shorts discovers that she has prescribed a contraindicated drug to an asthmatic. Should he:

- immediately telephone the patient?

- tell Dr Snow–Whyte to telephone the patient?

- set pharmacology homework and organise a test?

- contact the Postgraduate Office for help?

- other (please complete)?

Everyone makes mistakes. Often the pharmacist will save our bacon. Most of us would telephone the patient as soon as an error came to light, and the patients usually appreciate our concern. If I can do it, so can the learner. 'Do as I do' is a policy that is easy to sell.

> Dr Shorts: 'Rita, did you realise that there could be a problem with a beta-blocker in an asthmatic?'
> Dr Snow–Whyte: 'Whoops!'
> Dr Shorts: 'Didn't you get a message on the computer?'
> Dr Snow–Whyte: 'I didn't see one. Perhaps I got into automatic mode on the keyboard, and cancelled it?'
> Dr Shorts: 'What will you do?'
> Dr Snow–Whyte: 'I'd better ring up straight away. I do hope they're on the telephone.'
> Dr Shorts: 'That's just what I'd do myself. In fact, I've had to more than once in the past. We all make mistakes – the important thing is to put them right, if you can, as quickly as possible, and to learn from them. That's the mark of the true professional, and patients are usually grateful for the trouble you've taken.'
> Dr Snow–Whyte: 'Thanks. That will make this phone call much easier for me to make.'

Returning to the question of the end-product of education (in terms of a fully trained Dr Snow–Whyte), it is my duty to use appropriate educational methods to address the deficiencies that I discover, whether these concern knowledge of drugs or use of the computer. In the vast majority of cases, the deficiencies will be amenable to education, or at least to the methods I have at my disposal. If I have doubts about my ability to help with a major problem, it is equally my duty to discuss it with a higher authority. After all, someone else may be able to help. Different expertise and experience, or perhaps just a different personality to mine, could be the answer. Rarely, a problem is so serious that consideration should be given as to whether or not the learner should continue in their intended career. Obviously this is an issue for the authorities, and the sooner the better from the point of view of everyone. Thankfully, most difficulties are much less serious than this. These can be discussed frankly with the learners themselves, and then with one's partners or fellow teachers, if necessary, before taking the decision to go higher up.

Sharing the teacher's agenda with the learner means sharing these ideas, too. This is how Dr Shorts handled it.

Dr Shorts: 'Rita, I know that you've come from an environment where you learn to cover up your gaps in knowledge. At least, it was like that for me, as a student I mean. Have things changed much?'

Dr Snow–Whyte: 'No, probably not.'

Dr Shorts: 'Well, you'll find that there's a different attitude here. As far as I'm concerned, gaps are no problem so long as you recognise them. I want to know as much as possible about your educational needs, so that I can help you improve. I have plenty of educational needs myself, because everything keeps changing.'

Dr Snow–Whyte: 'I'm sure you're just *saying* that, Dr Shorts!'

Dr Shorts: 'Not at all, and I'll prove it to you. If we go through a multiple-choice paper together, you'll see how many facts I've forgotten.'

Dr Snow–Whyte: 'And you'll see how many I never even knew!'

Dr Shorts: 'Well, if we decide to do that, I won't be as interested in the score as in the pattern of deficiencies. As far as I'm concerned, it isn't an exam. There are other ways of finding out your knowledge base, but this is about the quickest.'

Dr Snow–Whyte: 'But don't you have to fill in a trainer's report about me? That's a kind of exam, isn't it?'

Dr Shorts: 'Well, at the end of the day, you have to be accredited as a trained practitioner, and my report is one part of that process. Look, here's a copy of the report I have to complete at the end of your training. If you look at the headings, they'll give you an idea of the goals that we should be working towards, at least in terms of minimal competence.'

Dr Snow–Whyte: 'Only "minimal competence"?'

Dr Shorts: 'Yes, that's all you need to get a certificate of vocational training. People just want to know that you're safe. There should be no problem, provided that you apply yourself reasonably. However, excellence is what I'd like to aim for, whether or not you take the membership exam.'

Dr Snow–Whyte: 'Yes, I'd like to aim higher than "minimal competence".'

Dr Shorts: 'Good. Well, the key to excellence is frequent monitoring of educational needs, using a variety of methods. I'll show you the file I keep. It includes a diary of problems arising from case discussions and an educational plan.'

Dr Snow–Whyte: 'Do I get to see what goes in that file?'

Dr Shorts: 'Not only that, but we'll agree it together first, and you can have a copy.'

Dr Snow–Whyte: 'This is amazing!'

Dr Shorts: 'Well, it's your education and, in any case, one of the main aims of training is to help you to manage your own continuing education in the future.'

Dr Snow–Whyte: 'But this file could be shown to the Postgraduate Office, couldn't it?'
Dr Shorts: 'Not unless there are extreme circumstances, and even then not without warning and lots of prior discussion with you. It's very similar to the relationship between a doctor and a patient. I wouldn't consider breaching confidentiality unless there were very pressing considerations, such as an uncontrolled epileptic who insisted on driving despite my advice. I've never had to use a file for that purpose. It's really for us, so that we can get the teaching right.'

THINK BOX

Do you believe Dr Shorts, when he says that there are no hidden agendas?

Do you agree that hidden agendas are a bad thing?

Is it really possible to eliminate them?

How are *you* doing in that respect?

Very often, the relationship between the teacher and learner, at least in the one-to-one situation, is extremely intense. By the end of training, they will probably know each other much better than patients and doctors or professionals and clients do. The sheer amount of time spent face to face is an important factor, but perhaps the main thing is that the health professional must develop self-knowledge and learn to use their own personality as a therapeutic tool. The personality and attitudes of the learner are thus a legitimate concern for the teacher. However, there are limits, and it helps for both parties to have some idea where they stand.

Contracts

If there is an employer–employee relationship (as there is between a GP trainer and a registrar), it is recommended that a contract of employment is drawn up at the beginning of the attachment. It is also becoming common for educational organisations to have *learning contracts*. In each case, the contract is a way of making an explicit agreement about important issues such as sick pay or time set aside for teaching. In the event of a dispute, the contract is there to witness the agreement that was made. The very process of making a formal agreement helps to clear up potential misunderstandings, and makes a dispute much less likely. If no contract exists, the parties may proceed on the basis of different sets of assumptions, and this may end in trouble.

It is probably impossible to cover all aspects of the teacher–learner relationship in a formal contract, but it does help to discuss the major areas and the expectations of both parties about them.

What about time-keeping, for example?

Arriving 10 minutes late for the start of morning surgery is a major issue for Dr Shorts, but Dr Snow–Whyte doesn't realise that because he hasn't told her. How many times should he let it happen before he berates her?

What happens if the teacher discovers that the learner is concealing an illness?

Dr Snow–Whyte is showing signs of depression which are starting to interfere with her work. She needs treatment, and possibly a sick note, but she isn't registered with a local GP. Should Dr Shorts refuse to get involved?

What happens if the teacher is intruding on the personal territory of the learner?

Dr Snow–Whyte realises that her attitudes are relevant to training, but she feels that her sessions with Dr Shorts are becoming like psychoanalysis. If only she knew how to tell him to 'back off'.

These are just three examples of problems that can arise, and which might be prevented by a prior agreement, even if it is only a verbal one.

Dr Shorts: 'Rita, we've already dealt with your contract of employment and the learning contract for the vocational training scheme. However, there are some other areas which we ought to discuss in relation to what goes on at this practice and how we manage our relationship as trainer and learner.'

Dr Snow–Whyte: 'You're the boss.'

Dr Shorts: 'Well, for a start, I like punctuality. If you arrive late, it puts pressure on the rest of the day, and the patients don't like to be kept waiting unnecessarily. Can you foresee any problems with that?

Dr Snow–Whyte: 'There's always a lot of traffic, and I live 20 miles away on the other side of the city. I will try my best, though.'

Dr Shorts: 'Why not start slightly later, then?'

Dr Snow–Whyte: 'That would really help. I wouldn't mind seeing one or two patients on the end of evening surgery to make up for it.'

Dr Shorts: 'Good. Now are you registered with a GP? If you are ill, it's best if I'm not involved in looking after you. There's too much potential for a conflict of interest.'

Dr Snow–Whyte: 'I understand that, and I have got a doctor.'

Dr Shorts: 'The next thing is a bit more awkward. It's to do with how we are going to relate as people.'

Dr Snow–Whyte: 'Oh, I'm sure that will be all right. We can see how it goes, and anyway I do feel quite comfortable with you already.'

Dr Shorts: 'Well, I think it helps to know where you are from the beginning, if possible. This job is not just about diagnosing illnesses and writing the correct prescriptions. It's about how people think and feel as well. How *you* think and feel is also important. We have to get into that area of the doctor's own emotions and personality.'

Dr Snow–Whyte: 'Yes, I suppose you're right.'

Dr Shorts: 'Sometimes it's difficult for the trainer to know where to draw the line. All I'm saying is – if you think I'm about to cross that line, tell me.'

Dr Snow–Whyte: 'Fair enough.'

Dr Shorts: 'I'd like to extend that principle to the whole of training, too. If there's anything that you don't agree with, please talk to me about it. We can probably come to some agreement.'

Dr Snow–Whyte: 'Thank you. That sounds really decent. Actually, I have got a few minor concerns I'd like to discuss with you.'

EXERCISE

Make a list of all the issues that have arisen during your own teaching activities, and that you wished you had discussed earlier with the learner.

What issues came up for you as a learner, that you wished you had previously discussed with the teacher?

I expect you've noticed that we're moving in the *nose* area of the *face* model – that is, the skills needed to reconcile the *agendas* of learner and teacher. The most important skill seems to be the art of negotiation (*see* Chapter 3), but the whole range of interviewing skills is relevant.

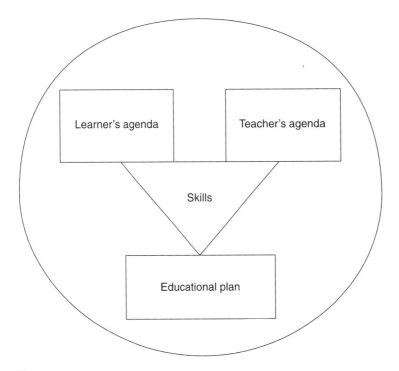

Figure 7.1

Everything in the interaction between teacher and learner is potentially up for negotiation. This includes:

- rules of 'the house'
- roles and relationship
- aims and objectives
- assessment of needs
- educational plan and methods.

The more thoroughly these areas are discussed, the less likely it is that there will be misunderstandings due to different expectations and assumptions.

Teaching and professionalism

The parallels between the relationship of the health professional and client and that of the teacher and learner are very strong. This means that the communication skills needed are to a large extent interchangeable. It also means that the personal element in the relationship, whilst very necessary, can get out of hand. Everyone knows that doctors and patients, or nurses and patients, can develop strong feelings for each other. If anything, the relationship between teacher and learner can be even more intense, for the reasons outlined above. In both types of relationship, the professional usually cannot escape being a powerful and caring figure in the perception of the client or learner. This often leads to a *transference* effect, which can sometimes be mistaken for love.

'I feel I can really talk to you, doctor,' says Mrs Fatale.

'Mmm,' says Dr Shorts, turning to the computer.

There's nothing wrong with feelings in themselves (*see* Chapter 4) but, as a health professional or a teacher, it *does* matter what you do about them. Being a professional in the area of communication means that you must constantly monitor and, if necessary, analyse the sources of your feelings. It also means acting in your client's or learner's interests, in preference to your own inclinations. Of course, feelings can be negative as well as positive. The professional should work to minimise their potential for compromising the achievement of shared aims and objectives. In extreme cases, if the relationship does not work, it may be best to transfer to another teacher, perhaps with a different personality. On the other hand, if the learner has serious personality problems, this should be discussed with the educational establishment at the earliest opportunity.

Perhaps I have been lucky, but I count most of the people whom I have trained as my friends, whether or not I have kept in contact with them. Nevertheless, I have tried not to let the fact that I liked them interfere with the professional job that had to be done.

'Sanctimonious, I call it,' says Donald.

'Perhaps he's just led a very sheltered life,' says Liam. 'I suppose, if you bore the patients and learners to death, there's not much chance of being hauled up in front of the GMC.'

'Having nil charisma has its advantages,' says Donald, 'but I am a bit worried about that Avenger fellow.'

Scene: The practice common-room, after evening surgery. Low lights are on and soft music is playing.

Dr Avenger: 'I'm so glad that you decided to retrain as a GP, Lee Ding.'
Ms Statistic: 'Do you normally open a bottle of wine to watch the registrar's video?'
Dr Avenger: 'I thought we might go in for a spot of formative assessment.'
Ms Statistic: 'It's not that so much as the debriefing that worries me, 007. So I thought I'd invite Sister Brasstoff along to keep us company.'
Dr Avenger: '*Touché*, Miss Moneypenny!'

An enterprising GP trainers' workshop group once wrote a booklet entitled *A Trainee's Guide to Training*. Near the end of it, the following question appeared.
What do you do when your trainer pinches your bottom?
And the answer was – yes, you've guessed it: *Turn the other cheek.*
Enough of this. I've made the point that therapists and teachers have a lot in common. The characteristics of 'the effective therapist', according to Carl Rogers, include the attribute of 'non-possessive caring'.[2] It seems to sum up the situation. However, inventing a slogan doesn't really solve the problem. That's for you, as we therapists say.

For adults only

Brookfield stated that adult learners have six main characteristics.[3]

1   They are not beginners, but are in a continuing process of growth.
2   They each have unique packages of experiences and values.
3   They come to education with intentions.
4   They have expectations about the learning process.
5   They have competing interests (the realities of their lives).
6   They already have their own set patterns of learning.

Therefore adult education is promoted by:

•   a suitable climate for learning
•   activities that seem to be relevant to the learners' circumstances
•   use of the learners' own experiences
•   involvement of learners in curriculum design
•   encouraging learners to be self-directed
•   facilitation rather than instruction
•   consideration of individual needs and learning styles.

You could argue that children should also be treated more like that, and there has been some progress towards this in schools with the introduction of ideas such as 'learning by discovery'.

'Typical sixties rubbish!,' says Donald. 'They're just in the process of realising that the three "Rs" have been neglected, in favour of all this airy-fairy stuff!'

Learner-centredness may sometimes appear to be a way of escaping responsibility, on the part of the teacher. There is, of course, a similar dilemma for health professionals who use the client-centred approach. However, the *face* model includes the teacher's agenda as well as that of the learner. Negotiation of the way forward includes sharing the teacher's ideas about the overall aims, curriculum and methods. They are, after all, supposed to be the experts. The learner's degree of involvement in educational planning should also be negotiated. It can be a 'culture shock' to be presented with the full adult learning package immediately after completing pre-registration training.

'There's no need for panic,' says Dr Shorts. 'Here's a curriculum I prepared earlier' (thank goodness I went on that structured trainers' course, he thinks).

This is all very well in an emergency, but how relevant is that 'prepared curriculum' to Dr Snow–Whyte's needs? Also, we have to keep in mind the ultimate aim of education, which is to produce an independent professional who is capable of maintaining their own continuing education.

Adult education should promote *deep learning*, which connects with previous experiences, cognitive structures and career intentions. Memorising facts and examples, rather than principles and strategies, is associated with *superficial learning*. Because it is less likely to connect strongly with individual experience, the latter is often short-lived. 'Pass and forget' is one way in which undergraduate medical education, for example, has been described. What we want is *continuing professional development*.

'Right on, man!,' says Liam.

Learning styles

Much of the theory about this is distilled in Patrick McEvoy's book.[4] Differences in the way in which people learn are very much bound up with their personalities.

- Dr Avenger likes to be up and doing, or bouncing ideas around.
- Dr Strait and Sister Brasstoff are only interested in what they can immediately apply to the job of seeing patients.
- Dr Shorts and Sister O'Mercy like to turn things over in their heads. You won't get a quick answer from them.
- Ms Toe is interested in models and concepts – and the more complicated the better.

Which of these does Dr Snow–Whyte most resemble, and does it matter? If Dr Shorts' teaching style is like his personality, will it be compatible with her learning style? Fortunately, most of us have mixtures of the different characteristics, which allows a degree of adaptability. However, it must be said that people like Dr Strait and Sister Brasstoff tend to get impatient with too much theory. Equally, Dr Shorts and Sister O'Mercy can't see the point of jumping in at the deep end, like Dr Avenger, before working out what it's all for.

EXERCISE

Suppose that you have to design an educational session on consultation techniques for each of the characters mentioned above (apart from Dr Snow–Whyte).

How would you proceed?

Would you suggest any preparation and, if so, what would it involve?

One of the best-known classifications of learning style is that of Honey and Mumford.[5] There is a questionnaire available, although it does depend on the learner's view of him- or herself. Four types of learner emerge (although there is considerable room for overlap):

- activists
- pragmatists
- reflectors
- theorists.

THINK BOX

Can you recognise yourself in these categories?

How much of a mixture are you?

Does your teaching style mirror your learning style (and how do you know)?

Can you recognise Dr Avenger & Co. in these categories?

Another view of learners (and teachers) is the serialist–holist dichotomy. I have had the privilege of observing a very striking example of this at home. My two children, who have opposite characters, both have piano lessons. One of them attacks a new piece head on in a great flurry, playing it right through. Although there are many mistakes, you can immediately recognise a shape, even if you don't already know the tune. The other one slowly practises the first few notes, with frequent repetitions, eventually moving further on in the score. For weeks it doesn't seem as if anything will be achieved. It certainly doesn't sound like a piece of music. The amazing thing is that both of them arrive at a similar point, although by opposite methods. Holists work from the big picture, whilst serialists are the step-by-step merchants.

THINK BOX

Do you recognise yourself?

How might this affect your teaching (and learning)?

Educational planning

The (mutually agreed) educational plan depends on negotiation about the agendas of teacher and learner, including methods of assessing needs. The programme is then generated by those needs which have been identified. Priorities and methods are also up for negotiation, the latter taking account of learning style.

From the point of view of good communication, as well as teaching, the learner's agenda and assessment of needs should be paramount (just as the client's or patient's agenda should be paramount in the interview), otherwise the subsequent action (the educational programme) might not be relevant. Thorough assessment of needs takes time, but it is legitimate to use designated teaching time for it.

Dr Shorts was worried about having to fill up a long educational programme, so he found a list of common subjects for tutorials from one of the books on how to train. The next task was to collect material for his tutorial file, so that he wouldn't feel at a loss in the event of having to prepare for any of these subjects. All of this made him feel more comfortable, but in the end he didn't have to use much of it.

All of the assessments went smoothly, after they had discussed the purpose of them. The multiple-choice paper was potentially threatening, but they decided between them to use the space of one tutorial to discuss possible answers to the questions, rather than sit it like an exam. Dr Shorts didn't know quite a few of the answers, although he was able to rationalise this by explaining that, for example, he didn't need to know the range for serum potassium as it was always printed on the laboratory report (he wrote some of his other weaknesses in the *reflective diary* that he had just started for his own *personal professional development plan*). However, it did emerge that Dr Snow–Whyte's main weakness was in the area of pharmacology. As Dr Shorts was sitting in on Dr Snow–Whyte's consultation at this stage, there was no need for video assessment. She related to patients, but had problems defining what the consultations were about. The use of drugs and consultation skills were clearly the main priorities, so Dr Shorts had to discard some of his immediate plans in order to deal with these.

As time went on, Dr Snow–Whyte progressed to consulting with patients by herself, and she had a daily debriefing with her trainer. Dr Shorts kept a record of the issues that were identified, as well as the action that was proposed to address them (*see* Chapter 10 on reflective practice). A few minutes at the end of each teaching contact were used to agree future aims and objectives. Sometimes, Dr Snow–Whyte found that she was given reading for homework, which she didn't mind, because she likes to think about things slowly. After a few weeks, Dr Shorts found that he had a lot of information about her needs, which had emerged from day-to-day practice. This triggered further teaching sessions, so that less and less room was left for his prepared list of topics. Another surprise for Dr Shorts was the willingness of his registrar to prepare for the topics they had agreed to cover. Evidently, because the whole programme was mutually agreed, she saw the educational needs as being relevant to her, and she was keen to work towards addressing them.

Here is a diagram of what happened.

Figure 7.2

'What did I tell you?,' says Donald. 'They all lived happily ever after.'

'Obviously made for each other,' says Liam. 'Groups, though, are a different kettle of fish.'

'*He* wouldn't think so,' says Donald. 'It's all about *agendas*, remember?'

A class act

Thank you, Donald. Of course, teaching in a group is similar to one-to-one tuition, except that there are more agendas to consider. Well, that is actually one hell of a problem!

The main difficulties arise from communication (*see* Chapter 6). The more agendas there are, the more potential there is for conflict. Also, it is more difficult for the individual even to be heard against a noisy background. The group teacher's role is to facilitate the members' ability to articulate their own needs, and to devise a plan for meeting them. It sounds so easy!

As explained in the last chapter, a democratic approach, with the leader providing facilitation, is probably most productive (and best in terms of the principles of adult education).

Dr Avenger: 'Well guys, what shall we do today?'
Chorus: 'That's up to you, 007.'

You can sense the expectation in their eyes. But just suppose the hero doesn't know where he's going. Mass hysteria could result.

Dr Avenger: 'Only kidding, team! Here's a programme I prepared earlier.'

Unless he's bluffing, the programme will help our hero to feel more secure, but not only that – the group will feel safer, too. Why is that? Well, a new group, fresh from a different style of teaching (not based on adult learning), will not cope with having the whole issue of designing their own education dumped on them at the beginning. That must remain the ultimate aim, but first the group has to 'gel' and, for that to happen, it needs to have confidence in the leader. It is a similar problem to the one faced by Dr Shorts and his registrar, but it's more difficult to assess needs and negotiate in a group.

Dr Avenger: 'Today we're going to play hide-and-seek.'

I think he's blown it. Looking quickly round the circle, I can see one or two significant non-verbal signals – people looking uncomfortable and embarrassed. Only his matinée idol looks can save him now.

Dr Avenger: 'Only joking! Actually we're going to have an illustrated lecture on the red eye.'
Chorus: 'Yummee!'

It's time to pass round the popcorn. To be honest, I expected more of him, didn't you? These charismatic leaders – they're all mouth and no trousers. 007 might have got away with it this week, but it's no answer in the long term.

Why *do* group leaders have people sitting in a circle, and why *do* new groups of GP registrars like lectures on the red eye? The answer to the first question is easy – because the leader doesn't have eyes in the back of his or her head. The second question continues to exercise my mind. Personally, I send red eyes to hospital if I'm not sure. Well, patients don't forgive you if they go blind.

Don't get me wrong. There are things I would like to teach my registrar about red eyes, to make sure that they practise safely. However, I would find it difficult to devote a whole afternoon to the subject, and in any case some of the group might know it already. So this illustrates the main problems in group teaching quite nicely:

*   discovering the individual needs
*   balancing conflicting needs
*   establishing whether the group is a suitable place for this teaching.

Quite obviously, discovery of individual needs is best achieved in a one-to-one setting. Dr Avenger hasn't got time to do all of the assessments that Dr Shorts is carrying out on Dr Snow-Whyte. It is possible for him to obtain feedback from the trainers' group about their registrars, but probably not right at the beginning of the course. When the feedback does arrive, the leader may wish it hadn't. Why should they all need the same thing? Obviously they don't. But wait – perhaps there are some common strands. Besides, Dr Avenger already knows what's good for them – lots of lovely consultation skills training. Bring on the actors!

Chorus: 'Aaaaaaaaah!'

That's the naked teacher's agenda, or should I say the teacher's naked agenda? Balancing the conflicting needs of the teacher and group members can seem like trying to square the circle (but have you noticed how that happens in groups, with circles always trying to become squares, preferably with a table in between?). It feels like time to let the group have a say. The trouble is that everyone's making too much noise. No, that's not right. Only a few people are, and I'm one of them. Now I remember – it's my job, as leader, to help the quiet ones to say what they think. How do I do that, 007?

*   Be vigilant – keep looking round the group to see who hasn't spoken, and who might want to. Be particularly aware of non-verbal signals.
*   Clarify group rules, including the necessity to listen to all members.
*   Make space – invite contributions from the quiet members and stop the more vocal ones talking in their space.

If in doubt, send for *Tyrannosaurus flipchart*. This is a tall predatory-looking object that is capable of dominating its ecosystem. It more or less guarantees the frozen attention of the group. You can easily make people talk *in turn*, whilst you stand up and write the bullet points on the chart. Hey presto! You have a list of points for negotiation, and everyone's had chance to contribute. One word of warning – if you want to progress to a meaningful discussion, get rid of the flip chart (and get them back in a circle again – they've been creeping into lecture formation).

Whilst we're in a negotiating mood, we have to sort out suitable methods for achieving our educational objectives. What exactly is group work good for? We know what it's not good for, namely dealing with a lot of individual objectives. Leave those to one-to-one teachers like Dr Shorts. Trust them to do it! There are two main advantages of group work:

- the opportunity to share a range of individual experience – for example, different consulting styles or approaches to the management of chronic disease
- the opportunity to use relatively scarce resources – for example, simulated patients, expert speakers or specialised equipment.

So there we are – with simulated patients and a red eye consultant! Experienced group teachers know what the groups are likely to need, and they know what works in groups. The tension between the adult learning and the need to provide a structure is always a problem, until you go back to the *face* model and remember that roles must constantly be renegotiated. Right now, the learners' agenda is that they need more direction from the teacher. Later, perhaps, we'll consider this politically correct stuff. It's sometimes the same with clients and patients. They just don't want the responsibility. If you don't accept that, you're not really being client- or learner-centred, are you?

Leading groups well is difficult. Teaching them as well as leading them is probably even more so. I've already said that you can't learn communication skills from books. This applies especially to groups, in my opinion. Practice in group work helps, particularly if you don't necessarily have to meet the people again! I would recommend attending a group leadership skills course. I hope the hints I've given you here and in Chapter 6 help you to learn from some of my mistakes.

You're a star

Yes, it's video time! The following approaches can be used either in a one-to-one setting or in groups. In the former, the situation is usually less threatening, and in the latter a large range of opinions can be canvassed. Various models of communication have already been discussed in Chapters 2 and 3, and dealing with feelings was discussed in Chapter 4.

Some people are permanently 'video shy', whilst others feel the same about the teacher sitting in. Video training has become universal among GP registrars, due to the requirements of summative assessment, and it cannot be long before these techniques become more widespread in other professions. What I used to do with 'video shy' registrars was to send them away to look at their video by themselves. I had assured them that I would never look at their video unless they specifically asked for help, although I would have to observe them by sitting in. However, if they needed help with a particular part of a consultation, they could show me that part of the video. Without exception, everyone showed me the whole of their video. In retrospect, I think they just needed to feel that they were in control.

- Let the learner hold the remote control.
- Agree on objectives and methods beforehand.

Here are the methods.

Pendleton's rules[6]

- The learner briefly clarifies matters of fact.
- The learner discusses 'good' points.
- The observers discuss 'good' points.
- The learner discusses potential 'improvements'.
- The observers make constructive suggestions.

This feels a great deal safer in a one-to-one setting, as the 'observer' is the teacher, and presumably tries to maintain a professional approach. In groups, it can sometimes get out of hand unless the leader is vigilant. The steps must be followed in order, and the leader must insist that any comments made by the others are constructive. Some doctors, in particular, are not skilled in recognising and valuing 'good' points. Consequently, they treat this stage as a charade to be gone through, before they can really 'put the boot in' (sorry, mates, but that's what it looks like to me).

'Sure, you smiled nicely when the patient came in, but the way you examined the cranial nerves was really awful!'

A good facilitator will stop this kind of nonsense. If so, Pendleton's approach is simple and works well, even in groups (well, most of them).

Calgary–Cambridge approach[7]

- The learner clarifies matters of fact.
- The learner discusses the perceived main problem.
- The observers describe what they saw happen (checking back with the tape, if necessary), avoiding value judgements.
- The learner reformulates the problem in the light of these observations.
- The observers discuss the possible options.
- The learner chooses different options and tries them out (in role play with an observer).

Learner: 'I couldn't get them to listen to my explanation.'
Observer: 'It looked like the patient was trying to ask you the same question as they did at the beginning of the consultation.'
Learner: 'Maybe I should make more effort to find out what they really wanted to know.'
Facilitator: 'Let's discuss ideas about how that might be done.'

This works very well in a one-to-one setting, except that the teacher must play all of the other roles available to a group. In a group, one of the members can be briefed to watch the tape from the patient's point of view, in order to be able to play the patient in the final stage. Groups who are already used to the Pendleton[6] approach tend to complain that the 'C-C' method is more complicated. Another frequent comment is that the whole approach seems to be more negative, because of the lack of emphasis on 'good' points. My impression is that they simply don't like being prevented from making value judgements (especially negative ones).

What I like about this approach is the way in which it focuses on the learner's agenda, and supports them in generating (and testing) their own solutions.

Neighbour's approach[8]

- The learner discusses the perceived problem, and clarifies any matters of fact.
- The tape is run again whilst the facilitator watches for signs of 'cognitive dissonance' in the learner (on the tape). The tape is stopped when signs appear.
- The facilitator explores and clarifies the learner's thoughts at this point.

Cognitive dissonance (internal conflict) means that the learner has an opportunity to deny the disturbing experience or to learn from it. This is potentially very powerful, but perhaps not very learner-centred. The facilitator stops the tape and focuses on something that the learner would rather escape from. Still, it must be good for you (whoops, another value judgement)!

If handled sensitively, especially in groups, this is a very insightful approach. At worst it can become like the 'third degree'.

Communication, teaching and learning

Teaching and learning is a major subject in itself (see *Teaching Made Easy*[9]), but communication is so intertwined with it that it is very difficult to draw a line between them. Ideally, I would have liked to have given this chapter an interdisciplinary perspective. However, although there are good arguments for making links between education for different disciplines, very little of this seems to go on at the moment. I've used doctors to illustrate the points, but I believe that the same principles apply across professional boundaries, having discussed the issues with nursing teachers as well. At least with regard to doctors' education, I can think myself into the situations.

As I see it, the *face* model fits well with the principles of adult education, and particularly with the notion of starting from the learner's position. Not only is assessment important in establishing this position, but it must also be 'sold' to the learner. Teachers often need to show leadership, and this involves sharing their own agendas with the learner. Negotiation is also very important in relation to the learning situation, roles, content and methods of education.

In groups there are many competing agendas. Therefore the educational plan may be very much a compromise, although many of the individual needs are best dealt with in a one-to-one setting. Leadership is even more important, and the group may need to know that the teacher has an agenda in order to feel safe, although the ultimate aim is still self-directed learning. Nevertheless, one of the most important tasks for the teacher is to allow all of the agendas to be heard and discussed. So much can happen so quickly that it is difficult for one person to keep track (in fact, a co-leader is often an advantage if one is available). The ability to detect and interpret non-verbal signals is extremely useful, and courses for group leaders are highly recommended. Despite the difficulties and challenges of teaching in a group, the facility for sharing different perspectives and the use of scarce resources are considerable advantages over one-to-one teaching.

Video feedback teaching, whether in groups or a one-to-one setting, is also challenging but potentially very effective. Skilled facilitation is needed to create a safe environment for learning. It often helps if the learner can stay 'in control', literally, by keeping hold of the remote control.

'Machines and more machines,' says Donald. 'They're more interested in playing with their toys than in listening to real people.'

'I can't wait until they have consulting by video-telephone,' says Liam. 'I hate trying to park near that health centre.'

What next? Virtual reality and the *face?*
Look at Chapter 8.

CHAPTER EIGHT

Papyrus to multimedia
INFORMATION TECHNOLOGY

Your contributions have been noted. I advise you to be careful.

Donald: 'What do you make of this? It's a note I've just received. Doesn't say who it's from.'

Liam: 'It's typed, so you don't get any clue from the handwriting. What does "contributions" mean, do you think?'

Donald: 'Maybe it's connected with the group I was telling you about (in Chapter 6).'

Liam: 'I thought you didn't say anything in that group.'

Donald: 'Well, hardly anything.'

Liam: 'But it must have made an impact! What about the last bit? Is that a threat or do they want to help you?'

Donald: 'I really can't imagine. You'd have to know who it was, something about their thinking.'

Liam: 'And reasoning!'

Donald: 'Otherwise, you have to take the message at *face* value.'

Liam: 'Boom, boom!'

Don't shoot the messenger

This chapter is about technology and communication – you know, computers, telephones, and so on. However, writing is also a kind of technology, although a very ancient one. Humans have used stone tablets and papyrus to record messages in the past. Now we're on to voice-activated word-processing software, but the principles have remained the same.

- Usually the sender of the message is somewhere else.
- What you see is what you get (however, the agenda may not be clear).
- There is no non-verbal communication.
- There is no immediate feedback.

Donald: 'That's silly! You don't get what you see!'

Liam: 'I wish I'd thought of that line! You don't get it – see?'

Donald: 'You do see it, but it doesn't help you.'

Liam: 'Aaaaaaaaaaah!'

Well, anyway, most messages are not so cryptic. You are receiving letters from other health professionals all the time and, by and large, you understand what they're saying, don't you?

Consultant to GP: 'We seem to have tried the entire drug repertoire on this chap, without noticeably improving his situation. However, there is a new preparation on the market called "Profiteeze", which has already been used a fair amount in America. I'm afraid I haven't a copy of the *British National Formulary* to hand in the clinic, and so I can't remember the starting dose. I would be grateful if you would just prescribe this for him, and I'll arrange another appointment in about three months.'

GP to Consultant: 'In the words of John McEnroe, you cannot be serious.'

THINK BOX

What do you think was the consultant's agenda?

And what was the GP's agenda?

Be creative!

EXERCISE

Look through your recent correspondence with other health professionals.

Can you find an example of misunderstanding that could have been avoided face to face?

What was the cause of this misunderstanding?

How did you deal with it?

What was the outcome?

On reflection, would you like to have changed anything you wrote or did?

I once went on an Open University summer school (not all my life is dull, you see) where I took part in a game about events leading up to the First World War. The group to which I had been assigned was confined to a room which represented one country. Every so often, written messages from other 'countries' arrived and we sent our own messages out. In no time at all, we were at complete cross purposes with the outside world and had our forces mobilised at the borders. It was a good job that there was no nuclear button to press. All this was highly predictable, I suppose, and the organisers were delighted with the outcome.

Communicating with other health professionals by exchange of letters can also get out of hand. Firing 'exocets' as a delayed reaction is no way to do business. The alternative, namely negotiation by post, is usually much too slow as it seems to take three weeks to turn letters round. If the situation is getting tricky, I usually have to telephone the person in question. At least the feedback is immediate and you can negotiate, even if the non-verbal cues are very limited. Better still is when you bump into the other person, say at a clinical meeting. Putting a face to a name is enormously helpful, and even if only a few words are exchanged this seems to clear the air like magic. Perhaps this is because you can better imagine the other person, the possible motives behind their written words, and their likely reactions to your own letters.

Having some kind of handle on the personality on the receiving end of your message enables you to anticipate difficulties (guess at their agenda) and to provide explanations in advance (that is, to make your agenda more explicit). This makes it more likely that the reply will be sufficiently constructive for you to work towards a shared plan. However, the lack of non-verbal cues and very delayed feedback associated with letter-writing provide ample opportunity for misunderstanding. Written communication can be speeded up by using the fax machine or e-mail, but specific arrangements will usually have to be made by telephone so that the messages can be received and processed quickly.

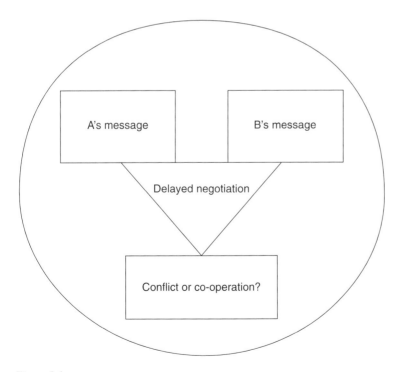

Figure 8.1

As clear as mud

Poor Donald doesn't understand the message I sent him. What was the purpose of it? Was it for his information only? Did I want him to do something, or not do something? Did I just want to scare the pants off him, for a joke? What exactly was my agenda? Let's try another message:

I don't like your contributions. Back off or beware!

That seems pretty straightforward, doesn't it? Except that he doesn't know who I am, why I don't like his contributions, what those contributions are, in what context, and what to beware of. So all he really knows is that the message is negative, rather than supportive. There's still far too much left to the imagination.

Here is another message from a hospital doctor to a GP: 'This man's hypertension is still not under optimal control. Therefore I have increased his Doxazosin to 2 mg daily. He will need his electrolytes checking in two weeks, before increasing the dose further if necessary.'

What should the GP do with this letter? Is it for his information only? Should he be doing the blood test, or has the hospital doctor arranged to do it? If the GP is to do the test, does the patient know this, and has the hospital doctor advised the patient to attend the GP's surgery for the purpose? Let us rewrite the message so that the GP knows what is expected:

'...I have increased his Doxazosin to 2 mg daily. Please will you check his electrolytes in two weeks and copy the result to the clinic, where I will review the dose on his next visit. I have advised the patient to contact your surgery to arrange the blood test.'

At least now the poor GP doesn't have to telephone or write to the patient in order to clarify the situation. Here's a message from the GP's practice leaflet to patients:

Saturday morning surgery is only for emergencies that cannot wait until after the weekend.

What is an emergency? What is truth? Who is my neighbour? Which of these questions is the easiest to answer? Ambiguous language is the enemy of understanding. To some people, an emergency involves blue flashing lights and nothing less, so they nurse their pneumonia until Monday and then ring up the receptionist.

'I'm afraid the routine appointments have all gone. Is it an emergency?'

It is still not blue flashing lights, but it is worse. What do I do now? Should I make a fuss or crawl away and die? Here's another version of the practice leaflet:

If possible, please try and see the doctor on a weekday, but if your problem will not wait till Monday, the doctor on call will be available in the surgery on Saturday morning. During the rest of the weekend the doctor will be on call for emergencies on the following number...

THINK BOX

That 'e' word is still there, of course, but do you think the message is clearer?

How might you improve it?

The following two sentences are taken from material derived from the Health Education Authority:

Most sore throats are caused by a virus infection which antibiotics cannot cure.

Tonsillitis usually starts with a sore throat which causes pain on swallowing.

What possibilities for misunderstanding can you identify?

How might these be overcome?

Similar kinds of misunderstanding can occur when people are trying to communicate face to face. Many of these are due to individual interpretation of the message received. What you understand by the word *virus* is dependent on your previous experience. I find that many people can understand a *computer virus* in terms of a fragment of rogue information, and this helps them to visualise what happens with viruses in their own bodies.

We are constantly monitoring the reactions of other people to the messages we give out, and this enables us to make fine adjustments – for example, when we realise that the other person doesn't understand the concept of a virus. Much of this adjustment is mediated through observation of the other person's non-verbal signals. It is easier to miss some of the cues when a third person is present and, with a group, you need eyes in the back of your head, especially if the group members aren't arranged in a circle. These signals are obviously denied to us when we send or receive written messages. Therefore it is particularly important to take care when deciding the content of the message, in order to minimise the potential for misunderstanding. With a leaflet that is going to be circulated to a large audience, this risk cannot be avoided entirely. The result is a compromise – some people will have a good understanding of the word *virus*, whilst others will have hardly any. It is worth asking yourself the following questions.

What are likely to be the predominant characteristics of the audience? What are their experiences and what are their likely agendas?

Having taken the trouble to find the most suitable words, make sure that your message is accurately produced. Misprints can alter the whole meaning of the message, and even turn it on its head. Michael O'Donnell, the medical broadcaster and writer, suggests that some typing errors actually enhance the meaning of the original, or perhaps reveal the unconscious thoughts of the writer. A GP received a letter from an eye specialist which ended '... it is probably not wise for her to continue to drive, and I have advised her of this.'

When the patient was shown this letter, and disagreed that it was an instruction to stop driving, the GP felt obliged to write back: 'I would be grateful if you would state this for her in clear *and equivocal* terms.'

What he had said on the dictaphone, was 'clear *unequivocal* terms', but I like the rogue version much better, don't you?

When it comes to audiovisual aids or written handouts for teaching, all of the previous remarks about messages apply. Presentation is arguably even more important here.

- There should not be more than two or three points per overhead or sheet.
- Make the points by using the simplest possible language.
- Use an adequate font size.
- Use variation of pattern and colour.
- Keep the whole thing short and simple.

Are you receiving me?

Ring ring, ring ring, ring ring, ring....

'Hello, hello. Is that the doctor?'

'Hello, this is Sister Matick, the triage nurse.'

'What's that?'

'I'm taking calls for the doctors' co-operative. How can I help you?'

'He needs a doctor, love. Straight the way!'

'Tell me his name.'

'It's Fred, Fred Bloggs. Can he have a doctor?'

'Yes, of course. Tell me the address.'

'Number 13 Nogoh Road, Mad Dog Estate.'

'Yes, I know it. Are you on the phone?'

'654321.'

'And who are you?'

'His wife, of course! Mrs Bloggs!'

'Okay, who's his doctor?'

'Avenger – but he's never there when you want him. That's why he's got to this state!'

'Can you tell me his date of birth?'

'Why do you ask so many questions when he just needs a doctor? Listen – he can't catch his breath!'

'Oh dear. How long has he had the problem?'

'I don't rightly know. Fred! – how long have you had it? What? Your breathing problem! What's that? He says he's had it years.'

'Is it worse now?'

'It's been getting worse all the time. Something's got to be done!'

'Anything else?'

'What do you mean "anything else"? Isn't it enough that he's probably got pneumonia?'

'What I meant was has he got any other symptoms?'

'Fred! Have you got any other symptoms? What? Have you got a pain or anything? He says no.'

'Can I talk to Fred?'

'No, he's in bed!'

'All right. I'll pass the message on to doctor.'

'Is he coming out?'

'Can you bring Fred down to the emergency centre?'

'I've told you, he's in bed, and I've got no transport!'

'The doctor can visit, but it might take an hour or so. We can see him straight away down here, if you can find someone to bring you, or even a taxi.'

'Well, I don't know. We're pensioners, you know. The doctor usually visits.'

'I know. Anyway, do your best. Let us know if you can come down. Otherwise I'll put him down for a visit. Can he wait that long, or do you think it's an ambulance job?'

'Oh no! He doesn't like hospitals!'

'All right then. Let us know if it gets more urgent. Is that all right?'

THINK BOX

What did you like about the way in which Sister Matick communicated with Mrs Bloggs on the telephone?

What would you want to have changed?

Why?

Can you imagine Mrs Bloggs' body language?

Can you imagine Sister Matick's body language?

What are the differences between a telephone conversation like this, and an exchange of messages by letter, fax or e-mail?

What factors are common to all of these methods of communication?

Making decisions about the management of a patient or client on the telephone is probably one of the most challenging tasks for the health professional. However, we are under increasing pressure to provide telephone advice because it is a more convenient service to our clients. It also helps to save us time on home visits and perhaps on consultations. This is difficult to prove, because the demand for healthcare seems to go on increasing. Why are telephone consultations so difficult?

- Face-to-face consultations are often difficult.
- Perhaps there is an expectation that telephone consultations should be simple because the phone is such an instant medium. There is a tendency not to take enough time, not to gather enough information, and not to record it thoroughly enough. These factors put the health professional in a vulnerable position.
- Although the medium is immediate, some of the feedback is missing because you cannot see the other party. Apart from the content of the message, all you have to rely on is the pitch and volume of the voice, and any pauses. This makes it more difficult to know how to 'pitch' your message, to interpret the replies, and to modify the message as you go along.
- No physical examination is possible.

The advent of video telephones would solve some but not all of these problems. Perhaps you think that's a long way off, but look how quickly computers have spread through many of our clients' homes. Professionals also experience difficulties in communicating with each other both on and off the telephone, but the principles are the same. As the challenges are probably most marked when dealing with patients or clients, especially out of hours, I shall stick to that situation as an illustration of the general rules. What the health professional needs is a plan.

1   *Introductions and rapport*: Say who you are, and find out who the caller is. Be friendly. *Smile*. Adopt a helpful and problem-solving attitude, however you feel (remember you're a professional).
2   *Essential data*: Patient's name, address and telephone number (in case you lose the call).
3   *Agenda of the caller*: What is the problem? What do they expect and why? Use empathy.
4   *Desirable data*: Anything else, such as the patient's date of birth and registered doctor.
5   *Verbal examination*: History of problems. Review of symptoms. Past history. Medication and allergies.
6   *Differential diagnosis*: What are the likely possibilities?
7   *Advice on management and/or negotiate place and time of face-to-face consultation.*
8   *Safety net*: Anticipate worst-case scenario and advise accordingly. Ask the caller if they have any questions. Check their understanding of and agreement with the arrangements.
9   *Document in similar detail to the case-notes, including the time of the call.*

THINK BOX

Bearing the above points in mind, how do you rate Sister Matick's performance now?

Do you agree with the telephone consultation plan?

Would you like to write down any modifications or write your own personal plan?

To what extent does the plan resemble some of the frameworks in Chapter 2 (e.g. that of Byrne and Long)?

I have always found the telephone to be a frustrating medium of communication, because I rely so much on feedback to what I say. If there is a relatively long silence, I tend to interpret that as disapproval rather than as some other explanation (e.g. that the other person is thinking hard about their reply). Some people are good at bridging the gap (left by loss of non-verbal cues) by using empathy. Making an effort to discover the layers of the caller's agenda helps the professional to be able to see the other's point of view and, in addition, to make the caller feel understood. A feeling that the professional is on your side, rather than a defensive 'us and them' situation, makes negotiation much easier. Also the caller is more likely to have confidence in any advice that is given.

The above telephone consultation plan is quite complicated, but ask yourself whether you can safely get away with anything less. Do not expect telephone consultations to be short, unless there is a quick agreement to visit or see the patient in the emergency centre, in which case some of the steps might be missed.

Big Brother

Computers are a huge distraction for health professionals. Instead of listening to their clients or patients or observing their non-verbal cues, the professional is busy staring at the screen or tapping away at the keyboard. You know what happens if you let your attention wander away from it for an instant – all of a sudden you've hit the wrong key and you're 'down a snake', and just as in 'snakes and ladders', it takes you ages to get back to where you were before. In the mean time, the patient is staring into space, trying to see what you are entering on the screen, or has resumed talking (and you're missing something vital), and now you're down another snake. Oh no! You've accidentally wiped the patient's notes off the screen! Here's an error message: *From Root Manager: Please log off immediately!*

Does this sound at all familiar, or is it only my own personal nightmare?

Not that these problems of being distracted were entirely absent when we just had written notes. I've seen many videos of doctors trying to listen to patients and read their notes at the same time. It never really worked. Below is my suggestion for managing the distraction element.

- Scan the notes (summary and last entry) and computer (journal and medication) before inviting the next patient in.
- Listen to the patient's account of their problems, without reference to the notes or computer.
- Save entries in the notes or computer for a suitable break (for example, whilst the patient is preparing for an examination), or after the patient has left the room.
- If you have to work on the computer (or notes) during the consultation, signal this to the patient. 'Excuse me while I deal with the computer. I'll be with you again in a moment.'

I know there are so many excuses for not behaving like this. However, just watch yourself on video. How much time do *you* spend ignoring the person who's made an appointment to see you?

So far, it's not much like Big Brother, is it? I mean the Health Police aren't actually watching you through the screen (switched off or on), are they? Well, don't worry because they *are*! Oh yes they are, you know. They're watching you and me, anyway – us health professionals. There's a Read code for everything, including how you like your tea. Mine's weak with no sugar, please. They certainly know whether or not you need remedial education about asthma management, just from the record of your prescriptions. Even at this moment, they could be preparing a hit squad to raid your home at dawn, and drag you away screaming to sit a multiple-choice paper!

For our patients and clients, it's hardly any better. I sometimes feel like putting up a notice in my consulting-room: *Be careful what you tell me. I might have to put it on the computer.*

That episode of 'stress'. Your visit to the 'special' clinic in 1964. Just you wait till I have to write an insurance report. But that's not all. Big Brother doesn't just store embarrassing information about you. It has an *agenda*, too. Oh yes! – ideas, concerns and expectations. The whole shebang! You see, it's not just a machine. It represents a third party in the consultation. A very big third party, in fact. Well, you can't get much bigger than the state, can you?

The state's agenda tends to be different to your own, at least in certain respects. After all, you're only one very tiny voter, and you're not even in a marginal seat. Let's take the example of antibiotics. You like them, don't you? They're the only thing that cures your sinusitis. Otherwise you're ill for weeks. Well, as you've heard, they're no longer flavour of the month as far as the state is concerned. And now your doctor is frightened to prescribe too many of them, because the Health Police have his number.

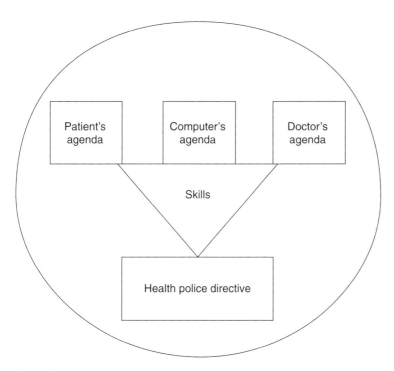

Figure 8.2

All right, I'm being very silly (I think they've started putting something in the muesli – Paranoid Crunch with added phenothiazines). In any case, there is a more positive side to information technology. It could support the consultation more, by providing information – not just facts, but probabilities, and even decision and diagnostic trees. Access to an adequate database would make specialist referrals for advice unnecessary. Big Brother could become our friendly expert in the consulting-room. To make this into a practical proposition, the technology would have to be improved, or at least be made more widely available. I can't wait for the time when I can bark at the computer, like Doc McCoy, and it carries out all my instructions without screening rude error messages.

Meetings between experts

Tuckett and colleagues suggested that patients were experts on how their own illnesses affected them,[1] but things have moved on since then. Expert information is no longer the property of a specific profession, if indeed it ever was. Our patients and clients are becoming increasingly likely to walk in, brandishing a printout of part of a learned journal they have downloaded from the internet. Not all of us feel positive about this state of affairs, but you can't turn the clock back. What are the problems of the professional?

They are twofold:

* the threat to the professional's role
* insufficient time to deal with the material.

I don't think you need worry too much about the first problem. Having information doesn't make you an expert. The punters need us to help them make sense of it. The second problem is a real one, because there is already insufficient time to do a proper job. Helping a patient to evaluate a scientific paper critically is just not possible, during an initial consultation, mainly because we don't have the time to absorb its contents. I ask the patient to leave the paper with me for a few days, while I at least read the summary. At the next appointment, I'm usually able to make some pertinent comments. To dismiss newspaper clippings and Internet files out of hand is akin to belittling the patient's own ideas. We shall lose respect if we do this. However, the time factor is still a problem (I keep writing to my MP).

Another aspect of *freedom of information* is that the records we make are no longer private. Many of us now write notes as if we were about to appear in court. Doctors' records used to be terse – for example, 'Bronchitis. Penbriten.'

This is an example from the late 1970s. All you see is a diagnosis and a drug. What we don't see now are the rude and supercilious comments that some doctors delighted in making. However, appearing in court is still an unlikely prospect (touch wood), so I think we are really writing for our colleagues, to help them to understand what we have been doing. Take the example above. How was the diagnosis of 'bronchitis' arrived at? Let's try again:

'Cough/wheeze – one week. Sticky white sputum. Generalised wheeze. Peak flow rate 180/450. Exacerbation of asthma. Prednisolone 30 mg daily x 7 days and review.'

This is much more useful for another doctor who might have to follow up. Here is how it is structured.

* Subjective information (e.g. symptoms)
  Cough/wheeze.
* Objective information (e.g. findings)
  Wheeze, peak flow rate.
* Conclusion (e.g. diagnosis)
  Asthma.
* Action (e.g. prescription)
  Prednisolone.
* Follow-up
  Review after treatment.

This tells another professional what you thought and why, what you did, and what comes next. It is also useful if you have to defend your actions at some later date.

It seems extremely likely that, with the advent of the 'NHS Net' and 'smart cards' that are capable of storing individual medical histories, our notes will become increasingly available to other professionals at least. Logic and clarity, as with any other form of communication, will therefore be very important.

The future

You've already seen most of it on Star Trek – hand-held scanners, talking computers, remote screen links. The future is here. It's mainly a question of paying for it. Remember, colour televisions used to be expensive. In the long term, the necessary investment makes sense, because the machines will act as instant consultants. Unfortunately, it is difficult to interest some politicians in anything beyond the next election. That's democracy for you!

However, when this revolution is fully realised, I believe that health professionals will have been given back their interviews and consultations. The machines will support – not hinder – better communication.

'Hallelujah!' says Liam.
'The man's completely flipped,' says Donald.

How are we doing so far?
Chapter 9 is about assessment.

How do I rate?
ASSESSMENT

'Assessment!,' says Liam. 'That sounds serious!'
'About time, too,' says Donald, 'though it's nearly the end of the book!'

We've already met assessment, in the broad sense, in Chapter 7 (on teaching and learning). Here we're concerned with *assessment of communication*, but similar principles apply. When a complex activity such as *communicating with people* is involved, it is often helpful to approach the problem from different angles. Each different approach has its limitations, but several approaches combined, such as the following, may give a truer picture:

- evaluation of written messages
- colleagues' feedback
- simulators' score/feedback
- consumer satisfaction/feedback forms
- evaluation of live interaction
- evaluation of recorded interaction.

Evaluation of written messages

GP trainers often make an informal assessment of their registrars' written communication, by pulling out a sample of records, referral letters and other messages. This method is applicable, with minor modifications, to learners in other disciplines. It may also be of use for self-assessment in your own professional development. The bullet points could easily be expanded in the form of Likert rating scales, although I have not used them in this formal way.

Client/patient records

The entries in the records are for you, other professionals, and sometimes the outside world to read. Do they have the following?

- Legibility, clarity and appropriate brevity?
- Respect for clients/patients and third parties?
- A statement of conclusion – what you thought was happening?
- Evidence for your opinion – subjective and objective?
- A statement of action taken – whether advisory or prescriptive?
- Indications and arrangements for review?

Letters and other messages

These may include referral or other letters, memos and entries in message books. Do they have the following?

- Legibility, clarity and appropriate brevity?
- Respect for clients/patients and third parties?
- A clear statement of the author's agenda?
- An attempt to anticipate the agenda of the recipient?
- Adequate background information (e.g. history, medication, etc.)?

Where appropriate, the last four points from the above section on records might also be included.

EXERCISE

Pull the last 10 records and the last 10 letters.

Check the last entries and the letters against the appropriate bullet points above.

Write a report with recommendations.

Repeat the exercise after an interval.

Colleagues' feedback

It is very common for trainers to receive spontaneous feedback (both positive and negative) about learners from other members of the primary healthcare team. This feedback can be sought systematically, so that the picture is comprehensive. It is difficult to obtain this kind of information about oneself as an established health professional.

Some trainers use feedback forms, such as the following (from the North Trent Assessment Package).

1 Knowledge:
  - of your specialty
  - of your role in the primary healthcare team
  - of specific topics relating to your field.
2 Skills:
  - practical skills relating to your field
  - appropriate use of referral to you.
3 Attitudes:
  - to you, and what you have to offer
  - to shared clients
  - approachability of the trainee.

The above items are scored on a five-point scale. Whilst they cover the whole spectrum of knowledge, skills and attitudes, communication skills are implicit in a number of them.

Simulators' score/feedback

A few words of explanation about simulators may be in order. The phenomenon of the simulated patient is becoming well known. However, not all simulators are the same. Originally, the scenarios and scripts for patient simulators were devised by doctors in an attempt to present a standard clinical challenge for students. Inevitably, the scenarios were somewhat contrived and the scripts stereotyped. At the University of Illinois, an expert medical panel worked on essential points (usually clinical) for each consultation that could be converted into statements capable of being answered by the simulator. Here are some examples.

'My blood pressure was measured.'
'I was asked about my family history of heart disease.'
'I was advised to stop smoking.'
'I was offered a cholesterol check.'

With a list of statements like this, validated by the expert panel, students could be given a score for each consultation without the need for a doctor to observe. This model was adapted by my colleagues on the Leicester Vocational Training Scheme for use with simulators who had been trained in a different way.

The Leicester simulators were recruited from local actors and teachers. First, they watched videotapes of GPs' surgeries (appropriate permission having been obtained) and noted down roles that might be suitable for them to play, particularly in terms of age and gender. Next, they met with the GPs and discussed the background of the roles they had chosen. The GPs then prepared a set of 'notes' containing the salient clinical points, and the panel of experts worked on a series of statements, Illinois style. Having studied the videotapes in depth, the simulators practised their roles with medical teachers, in order to iron out any problems.

The result was a simulated patient with a feeling of reality, due to internalisation of the role – in other words, real people with human ambiguities but internal consistency. The other innovation from Leicester was a simulator's feedback form which enabled the patient's point of view to be expressed. For example: 'I would/would not go and see this doctor again.'

This method of producing simulations can be applied to many forms of interaction – for example, between colleagues, and during appraisal or feedback. Although reliability has been demonstrated, there have been some criticisms of validity, as some clinical situations are currently excluded from the simulators' repertoire. Nevertheless, if the 'Leicester-style' simulators are available in your area, they are a valuable formative as well as summative assessment tool. One of their useful attributes is the ability to give informal feedback in role, and then to be 'rewound' to a previous point in the consultation so that another (or the same) doctor can try a different approach.

Consumers' satisfaction/feedback

Asking the clients or patients what they thought of the interview is an indirect way of assessing communication. This can be done by using interviews, but it is expensive and analysis is complicated. Satisfaction or feedback questionnaires are cheap and they produce quick answers.

Many satisfaction questionnaires have been produced, often for the purpose of relatively small studies of specific populations. Wilkin and colleagues reviewed them and concluded that the only one which satisfies strict reliability and validity criteria in the United Kingdom is Richard Baker's *Consultation Satisfaction Questionnaire (CSQ)*.[1] This contains the following four independent factors:

- general satisfaction
- perceived competence
- depth of relationship
- perceived time.

The CSQ and instructions for calculating scores can be found in Appendix 2.

Howie and colleagues, in Edinburgh, have devised and tested a simple measure of *patient empowerment* in a large pilot study.[2] They argue that this may be able to be used as a proxy for 'quality' in the consultation, and that it may also correlate with patient satisfaction.

Patient Empowerment Questionnaire (PEQ)

As a result of your visit to the doctor today, do you feel you are:

	Much better	Better	Same or less
Able to cope with life?			
Able to understand your illness?			
Able to cope with your illness?			
Able to keep yourself healthy?			

	Much more	More	Same or less
Confident about your health?			
Able to help yourself?			

EXERCISE

Try using the CSQ and PEQ for 10 to 20 of your consultations or interviews. Write an explanatory leaflet for your clients/patients to read beforehand. This should explain the purpose, who will analyse the responses, what will happen to the forms and how anonymity will be maintained.

Analyse the responses.

What have you learned about yourself?

What is your action plan?

Evaluation of live interaction

This requires one or more other observers with the required expertise. If they are observing through a one-way mirror, or sitting mutely in the room, there is not much advantage over watching videotapes retrospectively. Similar rating scales can be used (see the following section). However, observers in the interview room have the opportunity to question the interviewer on the spot, in order to find out what their thought processes are at that particular moment. Obviously this is potentially disruptive to the interaction, and the same questions could be asked from the videotape, but the answers will be fresh.

The technique of stopping the consultation and asking the doctor about their thoughts and reasoning is central to the use of the Leicester Assessment Package (LAP), which was developed by the Department of General Practice.[3] The reliability and validity of this instrument have been demonstrated in the UK and in Kuwait. Its main strength is that it produces a detailed breakdown and prescription for change in relation to the whole range of clinical and consulting skills. The drawbacks are cost (the need for two highly trained observers scoring eight consultations), the effects of third-party interventions in consultations, and the reluctance of some doctors to have their performances analysed. Although the LAP is particularly orientated towards doctors' clinical method, communication skills are interwoven with the 'small print' of most of the competencies, and are a major part of the first and the fifth ones.

Leicester Assessment Package[3]

The competencies to be scored, with relative percentage weightings, are as follows:

Interviewing/history taking (20%)

Introduces self to patients; puts patients at ease; allows patients to elaborate, presenting problem fully; listens attentively; seeks clarification of words used by patients as appropriate; phrases questions simply and clearly; uses silence appropriately; recognises patients' verbal and non-verbal cues; identifies patients' reasons for consultation; elicits relevant and specific information from patients and/or their records to help distinguish between working diagnoses; considers physical, social and psychological factors as appropriate; exhibits well-organised approach to information-gathering.

Physical examination (10%)

Performs examination and elicits physical signs correctly and sensitively; uses the instruments commonly used in family practice in a competent and sensitive manner.

Patient management (20%)

Formulates management plans appropriate to findings and circumstances in collaboration with patients; makes discriminating use of investigations, referral and drug therapy; is prepared to use time appropriately; demonstrates understanding of the importance of reassurance and explanation and uses clear and understandable language; checks patients' level of understanding; arranges appropriate follow-up; attempts to modify help-seeking behaviour of patients as appropriate.

Problem solving (20%)

Generates appropriate working diagnoses or identifies problem(s) depending on circumstances; seeks relevant and discriminating physical signs to help confirm or refute working diagnoses; correctly interprets and applies information obtained from patient records, history, physical examination and investigations; is capable of applying knowledge of basic, behavioural and clinical sciences to the identification, management and solution of patients' problems; is capable of recognising limits of personal competence and acting accordingly.

Behaviour/relationship with patients (10%)

Maintains friendly but professional relationship with patients with due regard to the ethics of medical practice; conveys sensitivity to the needs of patients; demonstrates an awareness that the patient's attitude to the doctor (and vice versa) affects management and achievement of levels of co-operation and compliance.

Anticipatory care (10%)

Acts on appropriate opportunities for health promotion and disease prevention; provides sufficient explanation to patients for preventive initiatives taken; sensitively attempts to enlist the co-operation of patients to promote a change to healthier life-styles.

Record-keeping (10%)

Makes accurate, legible and appropriate record of every doctor–patient contact and referral. The minimum information recorded should include date of consultation, relevant history and examination findings, any measurement carried out (e.g. blood pressure, peak flow, weight, etc.), the diagnosis/problem (preferably 'boxed'), outline of management plan, investigations ordered and follow-up arrangements. If a prescription is issued, the name(s) of the drug(s), dose, quantity provided and special precautions intimated to the patient should be recorded.

The scoring ranges from A (top level) to E (clearly unacceptable), with C being at the basic acceptable level. I have included the detail of this method because it constitutes a comprehensive list of skills, many of which have been discussed in the preceding chapters. Some of these, of course, are mainly appropriate for doctors, but many are applicable to other members of the primary healthcare team.

Notwithstanding the previous remarks about non-participant observation, GP trainers often use a mixture of this with minimal participation when sitting in with their new registrars. Notes on the points that arise can form part of their informal assessment. One situation in which the non-participant observer has a real advantage over a video recording is in a group. The video camera has at worst an inflexible point of view and at best a selective one, compared to an observer. The latter can quickly scan the group and focus attention on relevant individuals at the right time, whilst keeping a weather eye open for the unexpected. John Heron has produced the following schedule for evaluating the style of a group leader.[4]

John Heron's system of analysing leadership styles

Tick the appropriate box every time the person speaks. Extended contributions in the same category should be given extra ticks (one for every 30 seconds). If the person changes category, even if no one else has spoken, then tick the new box. Make a note of any non-verbal signals.

Authoritative

1   Prescriptive – giving advice/direction, being critical/evaluative, offering judgements.
2   Informative – giving information/interpretation, being didactic.
3   Confronting – directly challenging attitudes/beliefs/actions.

Facilitative

4   Cathartic – releasing tension, encouraging laughter/other emotions.
5   Catalytic – eliciting information, encouraging self-directed problem-solving, being reflective.
6   Supportive – being approving/confirming/validating.

Calculate the authoritative/facilitative ratio.

A basic 'catalytic' strategy for facilitating interaction combines complete attention, reflection, selective reflection, checking for understanding, and asking the types of questions which develop the other person's thinking.

An alternative template for group leadership skills comes from the South East Thames Evaluation Pack.[5]

South East Thames group leader rating scale

The tutor:

1   is personally open
2   encourages trust
3   facilitates discussion
4   inhibits loquacious locution

5   focuses on the task
6   recognises the feelings of others – verbal and non-verbal
7   recognises group process
8   understands group process
9   is able to reflect the group process back to the group
10   co-ordinates with other tutors
11   contributes to the development of the course
12   is able to vary the pace
13   allows process to happen
14   can hand over control to the group
15   can take control if necessary.

The above points are scored on a five-point Likert scale.

Evaluation of recorded interaction

The videotape is preferable for face-to-face interactions, as it records non-verbal behaviour. However, audiotapes come into their own in the case of the telephone. All recording is subject to the informed consent of the other party (see Appendix 1).

Telephone interactions

A taped record of telephone consultations is likely to become the norm in public services. If the facilities are unavailable on your telephone, you could set up a cassette recorder next to the telephone while you speak. Obviously, this will record only your side of the conversation, but you can often fill in the gaps for the other party's responses from memory. Use the framework from Chapter 8 as a basis for assessment, although it may require adaptation for non-medical consultations. Thus the following points should be covered:

1   introductions and rapport
2   essential data – especially address and telephone number (before they ring off)
3   caller's agenda (what do they want and why?)
4   desirable data (other administrative details)
5   verbal examination
6   exploration of options (differential diagnosis, if appropriate)
7   decision-making
8   safety-netting
9   documentation.

Face-to-face consultations

The consultation model of Pendleton and colleagues[6] (*see* Chapter 2) is also associated with a five-point Likert rating scale based on the seven tasks. This has formed the basis for a number of similar video assessment instruments, including the following one from the Sheffield Vocational Training Scheme.[7]

Sheffield Consultation Rating Scale

Good opening	Poor opening
Rapport established	No rapport
Reason for attendance clear	Reason for attendance unclear
Patient's fears/expectations explored where appropriate	Patient given no chance to voice fears/expectations
Appropriate history and examination (including social/psychological and medical aspects	History and examination inappropriate or deficient
At risk/chronic problems considered if appropriate	At risk/chronic problems not considered
Preventative/screening opportunities taken	Preventative/screening opportunities not taken
Results/diagnosis discussed appropriately	Results/diagnosis not discussed
Plan of management reached and agreed	No clear management plans discussed
Satisfactory termination of consultation	Unsatisfactory termination

In this scale, instead of a Likert score, a mark is simply made on the continuous line that joins the two opposing statements.

Pendleton's team also devised a consultation mapping system, again based on their model.[6] This enables the assessor to show how different tasks are tackled (or avoided) as the consultation proceeds. The tasks are listed on the y axis, and plotted against time (in minutes) on the x axis. The points are then joined up in a jagged line, which often resembles the temperature chart at the bottom of a patient's bed. Sometimes the chart is a graphic illustration of how missing tasks (such as not attending to the patient's beliefs) can be at the root of dysfunctional interactions.

Consultation map (Pendleton *et al.*)[6]

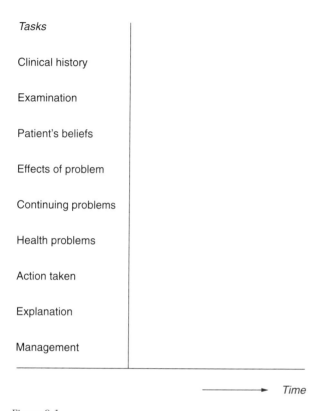

Tasks
Clinical history
Examination
Patient's beliefs
Effects of problem
Continuing problems
Health problems
Action taken
Explanation
Management

Time

Figure 9.1

Two further instruments, which have many similarities with Pendleton's model in particular, are used for formal GP examinations. Both require the examinee to present a consultation log. The first instrument was designed to measure minimal competence in the consultation, and is used in summative assessment of GP registrars, to assure safety in independent practice.

West of Scotland video assessment

Criteria

1   Error(s) – the presence of a single major error during the consultation or of a number of minor errors should lead to consideration of referral (serious error = causes actual/potential harm; minor error = inconvenience only).

2   Listening – identify and elucidate reason(s) for attendance. A credible/acceptable plan should be negotiated.

3   Action – appropriate action to identify patient's problems. Reasonable investigations/referrals are needed. Help should be sought when necessary. Patient's problems should be managed appropriately.

4   Understanding – registrar understands process/outcome of consultation. Actions explained. Obvious shortcomings identified and relevant background mentioned.

Rating scale

1   Refer.
2   Probably refer.
3   Bare pass.
4   Competent.
5   Good.
6   Excellent.

Overall assessment

•   R+, clear refer.
•   R, refer.
•   P, pass.
•   P+, clear pass.

Although there is a ranking score available, the instrument has been validated for the purpose of establishing minimal competence (i.e. pass or fail), provided that the statutory number of consultations and two levels of trained assessors are used. Second-level assessors deal with referrals from the first-level process.

The second instrument, which has been validated to produce a ranking score, is intended to measure excellence as part of the examination for membership of the Royal College of General Practitioners.[9]

MRCGP video criteria

1   Discover the reason for the patient's attendance.
     (a)   Elicit the patient's account of the symptom(s) which made him/her turn to the doctor.
           The doctor encourages the patient's contribution at appropriate points in the consultation.
           Cues that are present are not totally ignored.

(b) Obtain relevant items of social and occupational circumstances.

Appropriate details are elicited to place the complaint(s) in a social and psychological context.

The doctor is able to establish the effect of the illness on work or home life.

(c) Explore the patient's health understanding.

The patient's health understanding is taken into account in enough detail to ensure that there is a reasonable probability that the consultation will be successful.

(d) Enquire about continuing problems.

Information obtained allows the doctor to assess whether a continuing complaint represents an issue which must be addressed in this consultation.

2   Address the patient's problems.

(a) Assess the severity of the presenting problem(s).

Problems of differing degrees of severity are differentiated and treated with the correct weight.

(b) Choose an appropriate form of management.

The management plan is appropriate for the working diagnosis, reflecting a good understanding of modern accepted medical practice.

(c) Involve the patient in the management plan to the appropriate extent.

Management options are shared with the patient.

3   Make effective use of the consultation.

(a) Make efficient use of resources.

The doctor makes sensible use of available time and suggests further consultation as appropriate.

Investigations ordered are capable of confirming or excluding the working diagnosis, and the costs are justified in terms of the refinements the results might make to the overall management of the case.

Other health professionals are considered and involved (or not) (e.g. referrals are made when necessary or appropriate).

The doctor's prescribing behaviour is appropriate.

(b) Establish a relationship with the patient.

Allowing for the nature of the consultation, the patient and doctor appear to have established a rapport, or the doctor understands why no rapport has been established.

(c) Give opportunistic health promotion advice.

At-risk factors are dealt with appropriately within the consultation.

4   Define the clinical problem(s).

(a) Obtain additional information about symptoms and details of medical history.

Sufficient information is obtained for no serious condition to be missed.

Verbal investigation is consistent with hypotheses which could reasonably have been formed; the doctor appears to be open to more than one possible explanation of the problem.

(b)   Assess the condition of the patient by physical inspection if appropriate.
      The examination chosen is likely to confirm or disprove hypotheses which could reasonably have been formed or is designed to address a patient's concern.

(c)   Make a working diagnosis.
      The doctor appears to make a clinically appropriate working diagnosis.

5   Explain the problem(s) to the patient.

(a)   Share the findings with the patient.
      Diagnosis, management and effects of treatment are explained.

(b)   Tailor the explanation to the patient.
      The content and language chosen are appropriate to what the patient needs.
      The explanation given utilises (without necessarily adopting) some or all of the patient's elicited beliefs.

(c)   Ensure that the explanation is understood and accepted by the patient.
      Efforts are made to confirm the patient's understanding and an attempt is made to reconcile the doctor's viewpoint with that of the patient.

You may have gathered that the important word in these instruments is *appropriate*. That is why you need trained assessors. Polish up your appropriate button and out pops the genie with your medal. This would, of course, be a medal for doctors, not for other health professionals.

Next is an instrument, derived from the *face* model, which removes the emphasis on clinical problem-solving, as it is intended to assess communication.

Video consultation assessment form (VCAF)

Criteria

*   The needs and concerns of the patient were recognised.
*   The doctor's agenda was explicit.
*   There was a management plan which related to the patient's and doctor's agendas.
*   The management plan was carried out.
*   Future needs were addressed.
*   The doctor used appropriate communication skills.

Marking schedule

A   Criterion was met at superior level.
B   Criterion was met.
C   Doubtful whether criterion was met.
D   Criterion was not met.

To be able to make a judgement on the basis of these criteria, a consultation log is also required.

Consultation log form (CLF)

It would be helpful to add the tape time after each response below.

*   What were the needs/concerns of the patient?
*   How do you know?
*   What was your agenda as a doctor?
*   How did you communicate this to the patient?
*   What was the management plan?
*   How was this negotiated with the patient?
*   What were the patient's future needs arising from this consultation?
*   How do you propose to address them?
*   What communication skills did you display in this consultation?

If the words 'patient' and 'doctor' were changed appropriately, the VCAF and CLF might be suitable for use by other health professionals. I expect you all noticed immediately that if you fill in the CLF, you are giving yourself a tutorial. It could easily be used for self-assessment, or shared with your teacher/mentor.

Teaching

There is a parallel instrument, derived from the *face* model, designed to assess teaching (particularly the communication aspect).

Video teaching assessment form (VTAF)

*   The needs and concerns of the learner were recognised.
*   The teacher's agenda was explicit.
*   There was a teaching plan which related to the learner's and teacher's agendas.
*   The teaching plan was carried out.
*   Future needs were addressed.

• The teacher used appropriate communication skills.

The marking schedule is the same as for the VCAF above. There is also a similar teaching log.

Teaching log form (TLF)

• What were the needs/concerns of the learner?
• How do you know?
• What was your agenda as a teacher?
• How did you communicate this to the learner?
• What was the teaching plan?
• How was this negotiated with the learner?
• What were the learner's future needs arising from this session?
• How do you propose to address them?
• What communication skills did you display in this session?

Assessment of communication

Whether you are assessing yourself or someone else, as a teacher or as a learner, it is helpful to use more than one method. This is sometimes called *triangulation*.

I am aware that this has been only a selection and not an exhaustive collection of methods, and that most of them relate primarily to doctors. However, I believe that many of them can be adapted for the use of other health professionals. I hope that we shall all be working in closer co-operation in the future – and that means sharing teaching, learning and assessment methods.

Four of the methods described (simulated surgery, LAP, West of Scotland and MRCGP) are in use for formal examinations, but the first two instruments are also being used successfully to give feedback for teaching purposes.

What is to be done with all of the information that can potentially accrue from the use of several assessment methods? How is this to be tied in with day-to-day experience, and the conflicting demands that shower increasingly upon us?

'Well, I'm just going to crawl under my stone and think for a while,' says Liam.
'Is anyone sane around here?,' says Donald.
'It's called reflection,' says Liam.

Let's *face* the final frontier.
We'll boldly go to Chapter 10.

CHAPTER TEN

I reflect, therefore I learn
REFLECTIVE PRACTICE

Liam: 'Shouldn't it be: "I shop, therefore I am?"'
Donald: 'No, that's the Clinical Governor.'
Liam: 'What?'
Donald: 'You know, the spy who "shopped" me!'
Liam: 'That's just not funny.'
Donald: 'Please yourself, I thought I'd get my own back, before I'm finally written out of the script.'
Liam: 'That might be sooner than you think!'

Suddenly, the picture on the wall swings back to reveal a television screen. The synthetic tones of the Health Police reverberate through the speakers:

Donald Giovanni!
We have come for thee!

Liam Porello crouches, terrified, under the table, whilst the Don is dragged down into the flames. Mozart's majestic and sinister chords sound and the curtain falls.

The reflective Dr Shorts

Are we on a different planet? Is it the same one?

You thought that this was a book about communication in primary care, so why the excursion into Descartes, George Orwell and grand opera, and where's the connection with clinical governance?

Surprise! Messieurs/dames. That's the name of the game.

Dr Shorts was surprised by the response when he attempted to break bad news gently to Mrs Fleming (*see* Chapter 5). She was impatient with the way in which he seemed to be erecting barriers with his questions in order to avoid or postpone having to tell her the result of her chest X-ray. He thought that he was being correct by asking questions to establish her level of understanding, so that he could tailor the message accordingly. He'd read the book, even starred in the film, surely, the *face* model couldn't have let him down?

Do you remember *cognitive dissonance* (*see* Chapter 7)? Dr Shorts' cogs were certainly out of kilter. The choice before him was stark – either to deny the experience or to learn from it.

Where *had* he come across the technique for breaking bad news? He could remember *chunking and checking*, but he felt sure that they had asked questions, on the video, before giving out the news in small digestible portions. It hadn't worked for Mrs Fleming. That much was clear.

The immediate problem was how to rescue the consultation. Fortunately, Mrs Fleming had metamorphosed into a simulated patient (or perhaps she had been one all along – working for the health police revalidation squad), and he was able to replay the encounter (*see* Chapter 5). The second time round felt better. First, he checked out his assumption that she was here for the result of her X-ray. Then he gave out a small amount of information (she needs more investigation) and took it from there.

Dr Shorts had been through a process called *reflection in action*. According to Schon,[1] experienced professionals operate for much of the time in their *zone of mastery*. Within this zone, problem-solving has become largely automatic and the process is called *knowledge in action*. Suddenly, along comes a surprise (like Mrs Fleming)!

Reflection in action

This consists of the following:

1   recognition of the surprise
2   review of the problem
3   generation of hypotheses
4   information search
    • from the client/patient
    • from the body of professional knowledge
5   solution.

It wasn't the end of the story for Dr Shorts. Being that sort of chap, it played on his mind. He couldn't just improvise a temporary solution and then forget it. Besides, he was a trainer. It was up to him to set a good example to Dr Snow–Whyte.

Sure enough, when he had thought some more, looked up the literature and watched the demonstration video, he realised that wanting to be given the bad news 'straight from the shoulder' was an important part of Mrs Fleming's *agenda*. He remembered, too, that *everything is up for negotiation*, including the roles to be played, according to the *face* model. In retrospect, the opening stages of the video on breaking bad news had always seemed unsatisfactory. Just who were the doctors trying to protect – the patients or themselves? Of course, they had used actors working to a script. Now he could see no reason why the patients in the constructed scenarios might not have reacted as Mrs Fleming had, instead of co-operating with the doctor's long-winded approach.

Whenever Dr Shorts had visited his own doctor for the result of a test, he had always wanted to know what it was straight away. Surely, a series of questions instead of answers would have made him feel that there might have been something to hide, quite apart from the sheer frustration of it all. Why should it be different for most other people? Whatever the truth of that, it seemed to make sense (and was in keeping with the *face* model) to establish as quickly as possible what the patient wanted from the consultation. He could try something like the following.

> Dr Shorts: 'Have you come for the result of the X-ray, or do you already know it?'
> Mrs Fleming: 'No, I've come for the result.'
> Dr Shorts: 'It shows that you need some more investigation.'
> Mrs Fleming: 'Why's that?'
> Dr Shorts: 'Because there's a shadow.'
> Mrs Fleming: 'Is it cancer?'
> Dr Shorts: 'It could be, but they can't tell that from an ordinary X-ray.'
> Mrs Fleming: 'Could it be anything else?'
> Dr Shorts: 'Yes, there are a number of other possibilities, including infection.'
> etc.

He was quite comfortable with the rest of it (the chunking and checking part). But what if this was a new idea? Had anybody already tried comparing the direct approach to the first part of the 'bad news' consultation with the tentative one that seemed to be advocated by the video? Fortunately, the practice was connected to the Internet. It was just a matter of finding the time to search the literature. Perhaps this would be the start of an important piece of research.

As far as the learning outcomes were concerned, he must:

1   quickly establish the patient's agenda about receiving the news
2   avoid frustrating the patient by responding to questions with more questions
3   give the news in appropriate stages.

The best way to check whether or not he was achieving these outcomes would be to capture relevant consultations on video, but this might be difficult in practice, due to their relative rarity. Even if suitable consultations could be predicted (for example, a patient returning for an X-ray result), permission to record might not be forthcoming. Another possible approach would be to use simulated patients and obtain feedback from them directly and/or from a recording. Dr Shorts was fortunate to have the support of an active trainers' workshop group whilst he went through this stage of *reflection on action.*

Reflection on action

This consists of the following:

1 review of the surprise and its solution
2 identification of new learning
3 generation of new questions
   • review of literature
   • audit or research
4 identification of learning outcomes and educational needs
5 assessment of outcomes (new or modified practice).

Mentoring Dr Strait

At the end of Chapter 3, we had packed Dr Strait off to see the GP tutor about his educational needs. The latter soon realised that he had personal needs as well, which were at least as important, and put him in contact with Dr Mentor.

> Dr Mentor: 'Thank you for showing me the video, Dai. Of course, I can see the places where you were getting into trouble. On the other hand, you showed great sensitivity to patients' needs in other places.'
> Dr Strait: 'Thanks for those kind words.'
> Dr Mentor: 'Not at all. You've had so much experience that it would be surprising if you weren't very skilled at communicating, and you *are.*'
> Dr Strait: 'So what's going wrong?'
> Dr Mentor: 'Well, it might be worth going on a consultation skills course, if only to reflect on the skills that you already have, and to be able to use them more consciously in difficult situations.'
> Dr Strait: 'Yes, I think I might enjoy that. It would be nice to get away somewhere, too.'
> Dr Mentor: 'I have a feeling that the skills aren't the main problem, though.'
> Dr Strait: 'What is, then?'
> Dr Mentor: 'Remember the beginning of the consultation with that art student? Something else seemed to be getting in the way, didn't it?'
> Dr Strait: 'What was that?'
> Dr Mentor: 'I think it might help if you could put yourself back in that seat for a moment. What were you thinking when she told you about her sore throat?'
> Dr Strait: 'To be honest, I was fed up with seeing people with early symptoms of upper

respiratory illness. All the education I've tried, over the years, seems to have been a waste of breath. I get weary of arguing about antibiotics and viruses.'

Dr Mentor: 'Yes, I'm sure that rings a bell with many of us. Still, I know you realise that presenting symptoms aren't always all they seem.'

Dr Strait: 'I really hate myself for this, at times, but you know what it's like. Monday morning – if you get bogged down, you're dead!'

Dr Mentor: 'Dead?'

Dr Strait: 'Once you get behind, you never catch up again. By the time you reach the end of evening surgery, you're on automatic – and that's dangerous.'

Dr Mentor: 'And is that often the case?'

Dr Strait: 'Yes, of course it is! I'm not the only one in that situation – you *know* that!'

Dr Mentor: 'Yes, I'm sorry to say – and there are many reasons for it. To an extent, I feel I've been there myself, at least somewhere like it.'

Dr Strait: 'And you've come through? I'd love to know how.'

Dr Mentor: 'I can tell you about my experiences, if you wish, but they may not be directly relevant to your exact problems. For example, the workload you've described – not just Mondays – I wonder whether I could cope with that myself, whether *anyone* could.'

Dr Strait: 'That's certainly the way it feels at this end.'

Dr Mentor: 'Well, I wonder if it would be useful to focus on the sources of that workload, and the way that it is organised?'

Dr Strait: 'Time and motion? That sort of thing?'

Dr Mentor: 'Time management is one aspect of it. Incidentally, there's a very good distance-learning package...'

Dr Strait: 'Yes, I've seen it advertised, but never had the time to do it.'

Dr Mentor: 'You do have to go back to the basic philosophy of the practice.'

Dr Strait: 'What do you mean?'

Dr Mentor: 'Basic values. Aims and objectives – what the organisation is trying to achieve, and why.'

Dr Strait: 'You mean *mission statement?* We've got one of those. Everyone has to have them nowadays!'

Dr Mentor: 'Whatever you call it, the important thing is to agree on what you want from your professional life. How to achieve it comes next. It's a compromise, of course, between the wishes of all the team members and what is achievable.'

Dr Strait: 'Tell me about it!'

Dr Mentor: 'You know as well as I do that it's all down to the relationships between the partners in the practice. You can't manage time if there isn't any. To what extent do you think that your problems are shared by the rest of your organisation?'

Dr Strait: 'To a very large extent, I think. It sounds as though we need to talk seriously about strategic issues, but there's never time at the business meeting. It'll have to be an evening, I suppose. My wife will be delighted!'

Dr Mentor: 'Are you having problems at home, as well?'

Dr Strait: 'How long have you got?'

In many ways, the processes of reflection in and on action, employed by Dr Shorts in relation to his problem with breaking bad news, are similar to those experienced by Dr Strait with the aid of prompting from his mentor. Dr Shorts was doing it for himself, with a little help from his friends at the trainers' workshop group, but Dr Strait's problems appear to be more far-reaching.

THINK BOX

What do you think of Dr Mentor's performance?

Use Pendleton's rules (*see* Chapter 6).

How easy do you think it was for him?

What training do mentors need?

In fact, many mentors have had no training at all. Does that shock you?

Desirable attributes of a mentor[2]

These include the following:

1   credibility
2   empathy
3   ability to share vulnerability
4   confidentiality/honesty
5   non-judgemental attitude
6   enthusiasm
7   tact.

For example, it was most important that Dr Strait was able to *respect* Dr Mentor. This includes the belief that the mentor has something to contribute from experience, other than the ability merely to reflect back the thoughts of the mentee. It was also important that Dr Strait should be treated with respect, in a similar way to patients, clients, learners and colleagues. These aspects of respect, I think, contain the seven attributes listed above.

Possible roles of a mentor

These include the following:

1   resource facilitator
2   challenger
3   coach
4   adviser
5   counsellor
6   role model
7   teacher
8   confidant
9   sponsor
10 networker.

There appears to be confusion about the definition of the role of mentor – for example, in relation to coaching or co-tutoring (between peers). The above list of possible roles shows that there is considerable room for overlap. This makes it perhaps even more important than usual that the roles and professional boundaries should be negotiated beforehand with each mentee.

The whole range of communication skills relating to one-to-one interaction (*see* Chapters 3 and 4) may be called into play, particularly counselling, negotiating and giving feedback.

Feedback

This should be:

* positive, or at least constructive
* descriptive rather than evaluative
* specific, with examples
* as immediate as possible
* invited.

THINK BOX

Do you have any further thoughts on Dr Mentor's performance?

What would you have done differently?

Have you had any similar experiences yourself (from either side)?

How do they compare?

Reflection or mirage?

Of course, there is a sense in which reflection in and on action is taking place all the time in an informal way. Perhaps there is less discussion with colleagues, and almost certainly there is less consultation of the literature. However, because there is no documentation of the experience, it is almost certain that much of it will evaporate into thin air. The reflection will turn out to have been a mirage!

Write it down!

That means you are more likely to do it properly, and you can refer back to it later. There are a number of different approaches available, or you can invent your own. The important thing is to do it.

Log/diary

I suggest that you use an A4 loose-leaf file. Divide the paper into three columns as follows.

Date/activity	Issues arising	Action
1815 Waterloo	Grouchy lost Blucher	Remedial map reading for generals
1999 Surgery	Breaking bad news	Look at video
1999 Surgery	Not connecting	Skills course
etc.		

This is very similar to the diary that Dr Shorts already keeps to record issues from teaching sessions with Dr Snow–Whyte. You will find that it doesn't take long to accumulate a whole range of possible issues for reflection. The next thing is to insert a summary sheet at intervals, say once a month. This can be used to review and prioritise your learning needs.

PUNs, DENs and critical incidents

PUNs are **P**atients' **U**nmet **N**eeds. For example, Mr Pickett had a leg ulcer which stubbornly refused to heal. Arising from these are DENs, which are **D**octors' **E**ducational **N**eeds. Of course, it doesn't have to be doctors (or patients). In this case, Sister Brasstoff might need education about the role of referral in leg ulcer management (Pickett by name doesn't necessarily mean 'pick it' by nature).

PUNs and DENs could be recorded in two corresponding columns, or they could be incorporated into the log/diary format above.

Critical incidents are a bit like collisions and near misses in the air. What we want to know is whether they could have been prevented, and how. What if Mrs Fleming's chest X-ray report had been filed accidentally, without any action being taken, and what if the patient then assumed that no news is good news? The action needed to prevent such a thing happening again might well be organisational rather than educational. Nevertheless, the principles are very similar to PUNs and DENs. It's just that the whole system might be nearer to melt-down. It also needs to be recorded, if the lessons learned are to be permanent. New standards should be set, and they should be audited.

Personal learning plan

Education for healthcare professionals can be haphazard, as it may be based on:

* wants rather than needs
* the provider's agenda
* convenience or the easiest options.

Here's how to base it on *reflective practice*.

1   Document personal educational needs by:
    * log/diary
    * PUNs and DENs
    * critical incident review
    * results of audit.
2   Reflect in and on action (with or without peer support or mentoring).
3   Document resulting:
    * aims and objectives
    * educational methods
    * assessment of outcomes.

The result is an educational plan which is truly personal and based on the needs of patients or clients. It will be more challenging to carry out than passive learning loosely related to need, but infinitely more satisfying. The introduction of *clinical governance* will make it a necessity for every health professional.

Portfolio

Suppose you could capture the essence of all of these improving activities, so that you could refer back to them for the rest of your professional life. Well, you can! It's called a *portfolio!*

Portfolios come in all shapes and sizes. Kerry-Ann has one of these large flat things with a handle on top. Inside it she keeps all her 'life' drawings. My father has a whole room full of books and papers, on which he has been working for the last few decades. Ask him almost anything about history or economics, and he'll find the answer for you in a fairly short time.

Everyone has to start somewhere, and a loose-leaf or box file is as good a place as any. You could keep everything, which is how many of us start, but you would soon need a larger house. Some kind of selection process is usually necessary. For example, do you really need to keep invitation letters and maps of the campus for courses you have attended?

Keep notes of the essential learning points, *those you wish to put into practice*, and any supporting material (or references to it). If your portfolio develops into multiple bulging files, or even a whole room, you will need to be able to find your way round it easily. I suggest a smaller file, containing a summary and directions. The larger files should also be organised in sections, for easy navigation.

The smaller file becomes the *portable* part of the portfolio. You can take it round to show future employers a summary of the following:

• your qualifications
• your competences
• your experiences
• your educational plan.

This phenomenon is much further advanced in nursing, compared to the medical profession. Health professionals should take every opportunity to learn from each other. Does Dr Strait even know about Ms Toe's portfolio, still less that he features heavily in it (as one of the barriers to progress)?

Full circle

The reflective process applies to all aspects of education for professionals, and not just to communication. Nevertheless, writing is a form of communication and, unless you communicate (if only with yourself), reflection of itself is ephemeral.

Use it or lose it!

The learning cycle also applies to education across the board.

Kolb's learning cycle[3]

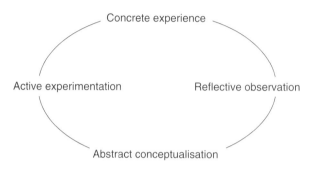

Figure 10.1

The 'complete learner' is said to be able to use all four stages with equal facility, but most of us have a preferred or dominant learning style (*see* also Honey and Mumford[4] in Chapter 7). Guess which mine is (here's a hint – don't ask me to tune the video, or let me near any other kind of machine, for that matter). The different stages of the cycle don't necessarily have to be approached in any particular order, so it doesn't need to be a cycle at all.

However, I did go round the cycle (clockwise) when developing the ideas which form the basis of this book.

1   My registrars were having problems with the final stages of the consultation.
2   I concluded that the roots of the problem were in the first stage of the consultation.
3   I devised the *face* model of the consultation.
4   I applied the model to everyday practice and teaching, and generated hypotheses for research.

You, too, can apply it to your own reflective practice.

What about Dr Strait, Sister Brasstoff and the rest of the team? They all read this book. And they all lived happily ever after in the new NHS, modern and dependable. No, it's not a fairy story – a politician saw the light and realised that the health professionals need support in order to be able to deliver *value for money* reliably. That means support for education, and support for better communication. What a happy ending!

Bibliography

Chapter 1
References

1   Neighbour R (1987) *The Inner Consultation*. MTP Press, Lancaster.
2   Neighbour R (1996) *The Inner Apprentice*. Petroc Press, Newbury.
3   Pendleton D, Schofield T, Tate P and Havelock PP (1984) *The Consultation: an approach to learning and teaching*. Oxford Medical Press, Oxford.
4   Stott NCH and Davis RH (1979) The exceptional potential in each primary care consultation. *J R Coll Gen Pract*. **29**: 201–5.
5   Byrne PS and Long BEL (1976) *Doctors Talking to Patients*. HMSO, London.
6   Laing RD (1970) *Knots*. Tavistock, London.

Further reading

Middleton JF (1989) The exceptional potential of the consultation revisited. *J R Coll Gen Pract*. **39**: 383–6.
Sartre J-P (1946) In camera (translated by S Gilbert). In: *Two Plays*. Hamish Hamilton, London.

Chapter 2
References

1   Erikson E (1977) *Childhood and Society*. Triad/Granada.
2   Hoffbrand BI (1989) Away with the system review: a plea for parsimony. *BMJ*. **298**: 817–19.
3   Byrne PS and Long BEL (1976) *Doctors Talking to Patients*. HMSO, London.
4   Tuckett D, Boulton M, Olson C and Williams A (1985) *Meetings Between Experts: an approach to sharing ideas in medical consultations*. Tavistock, London.
5   Berne E (1964) *Games People Play*. Penguin Books, Harmondsworth.
6   Stott NCH and Davis RH (1979) The exceptional potential in each primary care consultation. *J R Coll Gen Pract*. **29**: 201–5.
7   Pendleton D, Schofield T, Tate P and Havelock PP (1984) *The Consultation: an approach to learning and teaching*. Oxford Medical Press, Oxford.
8   Neighbour R (1987) *The Inner Consultation*. MTP Press, Lancaster.
9   Noakes J (1990) Double agent. *Br J Gen Pract*. **40**: 92–3.
10 Middleton JF (1989) The exceptional potential of the consultation revisited. *J R Coll Gen Pract*. **39**: 383–6.

11   Middleton JF (1991) Successful consultations: the patient's agenda. *Mod Med.* **April:** 183–6.

12   Middleton JF (1991) The doctor's agenda in the successful consultation. *Mod Med.* **May:** 245–7.

13   Roper N, Logan WW and Tierney AJ (1985) *The Elements of Nursing* (2e). Churchill Livingstone, Edinburgh.

14   Kershaw B and Salvage J (eds) (1986) *Models for Nursing.* John Wiley, Chichester.

15   Bendix T (1982) *The Anxious Patient: the therapeutic dialogue in clinical practice.* Churchill Livingstone, Edinburgh.

16   Helman CG (1981) Disease versus illness in general practice. *J R Coll Gen Pract.* **31:** 548–52.

17   Beckman HB, Frankel RM and Darnley J (1985) Soliciting the patient's complete agenda: a relationship to the distribution of concerns. *Clin Res.* **33 (Supplement)**: 714A.

18   Stewart MA, McWhinney IR and Buck CW (1975) How illness presents: a study of patient behaviour. *J Fam Pract.* **2:** 411–14.

19   Cartwright A and Anderson R (1981) *General Practice Revisited.* Tavistock. London.

20   Cromarty I (1996) What do patients think about during their consultations? A qualitative study. *Br J Gen Pract.* **46:** 525–8.

21   Beckman HB and Frankel RM (1984) The effect of physician behaviour on the collection of data. *Ann Intern Med.* **107:** 692–6.

Further reading

Elstein AS, Shulman LS and Sprafka SI (1978) *Medical Problem Solving: an analysis of clinical reasoning.* Harvard University Press, Cambridge, MA.

McAvoy BR (1999) In: R Fraser (ed) *Clinical Method: a general practice approach* (3e). Butterworth-Heinemann, Oxford.

Stott NCH (1993) When something is good, more of the same is not always better. William Pickles Lecture. *Br J Gen Pract.* **43:** 254–8.

Chapter 3
References

1   Neighbour R (1987) *The Inner Consultation.* MTP Press, Lancaster.

2   Neighbour R (1996) *The Inner Apprentice.* Petroc Press, Newbury.

3   Pendleton D, Schofield T, Tate P and Havelock PP (1984) *The Consultation: an approach to learning and teaching.* Oxford Medical Press, Oxford.

4   Roper N, Logan WW and Tierney AJ (1985) *The Elements of Nursing* (2e). Churchill Livingstone, Edinburgh.

5   Berne E (1964) *Games People Play.* Penguin Books, Harmondsworth.

6   Erikson E (1977) *Childhood and Society.* Triad/Granada.

7   Byrne PS and Long BEL (1976) *Doctors Talking to Patients.* HMSO, London.

8   Silverman J, Kurtz S and Draper J (1998) *Skills for Communicating with Patients.* Radcliffe Medical Press, Oxford.

Further reading

Argyle M (1972) *The Psychology of Interpersonal Behaviour* (2e). Pitman, London.

Corney R (ed) (1991) *Developing Communication and Counselling Skills in Medicine*. Routledge, London.

Heath C (1986) *Body Movement and Speech in Medical Interaction*. Cambridge University Press, Cambridge.

Kurtz S, Silverman J and Draper J (1998) *Teaching and Learning Communication Skills in Medicine*. Radcliffe Medical Press, Oxford.

Middleton JF (1989) The exceptional potential of the consultation revisited. *J R Coll Gen Pract*. **39**: 383–6.

Middleton JF (1991) The doctor's agenda in the successful consultation. *Mod Med*. **May**: 245–7.

Middleton JF (1990) How trainees learn. *Horizons*. **July**: 409–12.

Tate PHL (1997) *The Doctor's Communication Handbook* (2e). Radcliffe Medical Press, Oxford.

Chapter 4
References

1 Rogers C (1980) *A Way of Being*. Houghton Mifflin, Boston, MA.
2 Freeling P and Harris CM (1984) *The Doctor–Patient Relationship* (3e). Churchill Livingstone, Edinburgh.
3 Berne E (1964) *Games People Play*. Penguin Book, Harmondsworth.
4 Berger J and Mohr J (1976) *A Fortunate Man*. Writers and Readers Publishing Co-operative, London.
5 Sartre J-P (1946) In camera (translated by S Gilbert). In: *Two Plays*. Hamish Hamilton, London.
6 Balint M (1964) *The Doctor, his Patient and the Illness* (2e). Pitman, London.
7 Freud S (1973) *New Introductory Lectures on Psychoanalysis*. Pelican, London.

Further reading

Balint E and Norrell JS (1973) *Six Minutes for the Patient*. Tavistock, London.

Freud S (1976) *The Interpretation of Dreams*. Pelican, London.

Middleton JF (1991) Teaching about feelings. *Horizons*. **March**: 97–100.

Chapter 5
Further reading

Buckman R (1984) Breaking bad news: why is it still so difficult? *BMJ* **288**: 1597–99.

Marson S, Hartlebury M, Johnston R and Scammell B (1990) *Managing People*. Essentials of Nursing Management Series. Macmillan, London.

Stein-Parbury J (1993) *Patient and Person: developing interpersonal skills in nursing*. Churchill Livingstone, London.

Chapter 6
References

1   Maier NRF (1963) *Problem-Solving Discussions and Conference: leadership methods and skills.* McGraw-Hill, New York.
2   Heron J (1975) *Six Category Intervention Analysis.* University of Surrey, Guildford.
3   Freud S (1973) *New Introductory Lectures on Psychoanalysis.* Pelican, London.
4   Bion WR 1961 *Experiences in Groups.* Tavistock, London.
5   Kindred M and Kindred M (1998) *Once Upon a Group.* 4M Publications, Southwell.
6   Bolden K, Dwyer D, Leete R and Steele R (1988) *Running a Course.* Radcliffe Medical Press, Oxford.
7   Belbin RM (1991) *Management Teams: why they succeed or fail.* Heinemann, London.
8   McEvoy P (1998) *Educating the Future GP* (2e). Radcliffe Medical Press, Oxford.
9   Janis IL (1968) *Victims of Group Think: a psychological study of foreign policy decisions and fiascos.* Houghton Mifflin, Boston, MA.
10   Lewin K (1958) Group decision and social change. In: EE Maccoby, M Newcombe and EL Hartley (eds) *Readings in Social Psychology* (3e). Holt, Rinehart and Winston, New York.
11   Hall J and Watson WH (1970) The effects of normative intervention on group decision-making performance. *Human Relations.* **23:** 299–317.

Further reading

Davis JH (1969) *Group Performance.* Addison-Wesley, London.
White R and Lippitt R (1960) *Autocracy and Democracy.* Harper and Row, New York.

Chapter 7
References

1   Sartre J-P (1946) In camera (translated by S Gilbert). In: *Two Plays.* Hamish Hamilton, London.
2   Rogers C (1980) *A Way of Being.* Houghton Mifflin, Boston, MA.
3   Brookfield SD (1986) *Understanding and Facilitating Adult Learning.* Open University Press, Milton Keynes.
4   McEvoy P (1998) *Educating the Future GP* (2e). Radcliffe Medical Press, Oxford.
5   Honey P and Mumford A (1986) *The Manual of Learning Styles.* Peter Honey, Maidenhead.
6   Pendleton D, Schofield T, Tate P and Havelock PP (1984) *The Consultation: an approach to learning and teaching.* Oxford Medical Press, Oxford.
7   Kurtz S, Silverman J and Draper J (1998) *Teaching and Learning Communication Skills in Medicine.* Radcliffe Medical Press, Oxford.
8   Neighbour R (1996) *The Inner Apprentice.* Petroc Press, Newbury.
9   Chambers R and Wall D (1999) *Teaching Made Easy.* Radcliffe Medical Press, Oxford.

Further reading

Hall MS (ed) (1999) *A GP Training Handbook* (2e). Blackwell Science, Oxford.
Scottish Council For Postgraduate Medical Education (1991) *Learning General Practice* (3e). Scottish Council for Postgraduate Medical Education, Edinburgh.

Chapter 8
References

1   Tuckett D, Boulton M, Olson C and Williams A (1985) *Meetings Between Experts: an approach to sharing ideas in medical consultations*. Tavistock, London.

Chapter 9
References

1   Baker RH (1990) Development of a questionnaire to assess patients' satisfaction with consultations in general practice. *Br J Gen Pract*. **40**: 487–90.
2   Howie JG, Heaney DJ, Maxwell M and Walker JJ (1998) A comparison of a Patient Enablement Instrument (PEI) against two established satisfaction scales as an outcome measure of primary care consultations. *Fam Prac*. **15**: 165–71.
3   Fraser R (1994) *The Leicester Assessment Package* (2e). University of Leicester, Leicester.
4   Heron J (1975) *Six Category Intervention Analysis*. University of Surrey, Guildford.
5   Grant J, Evans K, May R, Savage S and Savage R (1993) *An Evaluation Pack for Education in General Practice*. British Postgraduate Medical Federation, University of London, London.
6   Pendleton D, Schofield T, Tate P and Havelock P (1984) *The Consultation: an approach to learning and teaching*. Oxford Medical Press, Oxford.
7   Chambers G (1988) *Trainee Assessment*. Sheffield Vocational Training Scheme, Sheffield.
8   Campbell LM, Howie JGR and Murray TS (1993) Summative assessment: the West of Scotland pilot project. *Br J Gen Pract*. **43**: 430–34.
9   Howie JGR, Heaney DJ and Maxwell M (1997) *Measuring Quality in General Practice*. Occasional Paper 75. The Royal College of General Practitioners, London.

Further reading

Middleton JF (1989) The exceptional potential of the consultation revisited. *J R Coll Gen Pract*. **39**: 383–6.
Rashid A, Allen J, Thew R and Aram G (1994) Performance-based assessment using simulated patients. *Educ Gen Pract*. **5**: 151–6.
Wilkin D, Hallam L and Doggett MA (1992) *Measures of Need and Outcome for Primary Health Care*. Oxford University Press, Oxford.

Chapter 10

References

1   Schon DA (1987) *Educating the Reflective Practitioner: towards a new design for teaching and learning in the professions.* Jossey-Bass, San Francisco, CA.
2   Morton-Cooper A and Palmer A (eds) (1999) *Mentoring and Preceptorship.* Blackwell Science, Oxford.
3   Kolb DA (1984) *Experiential Learning Experience as a Source of Learning and Development.* Prentice Hall, New York.
4   Honey P and Mumford A (1986) *The Manual of Learning Styles.* Peter Honey, Maidenhead.

Further reading

Royal College of General Practitioners (1989) *If Only I Had the Time.* Distance-learning package. Royal College of General Practitioners, London.
Royal College of General Practitioners (1994) *Portfolio-based Learning in General Practice.* Occasional Paper 63. Royal College of General Practitioners, London.
Royal College of General Practitioners (1996) *Significant Event Auditing.* Occasional Paper 70. Royal College of General Practitioners, London.

Appendices

Appendix 1: Video Consent Form
Appendix 2: CSQ and scoring instructions
Reproduced by kind permission of the author, Professor Richard Baker (Director of the Clinical Governance Unit, University of Leicester) – *see* Bibliography for Chapter 9.

Appendix 1

VIDEO CONSENT FORM

[DATE............../.............../..............]

NAME OF CONSULTING DOCTOR...

NAME OF PATIENT ....

NAMES OF PERSONS ACCOMPANYING PATIENT TO CONSULTATION:

....

Dr .... is making a video of his/her consultations. Intimate physical examinations will not be recorded and the camera will be switched off on request.

The tape will be used for the purposes of assessment of the doctor, research, learning and teaching purposes. It will be seen only by persons who have legal access to your medical records.

Dr .... is responsible for the security and confidentiality of the video recording. If the tape is to leave the practice premises it will be sent by registered post or personal messenger.

Delete (a) or (b) as appropriate.

(a) Today's recording will be seen only by doctors within the practice and will be erased as soon as it has been studied and not later than one year from the date of recording.

(b) Today's recording will be inside your practice but it may also need to be seen outside the practice by people appointed to judge the standards of your doctor. The tape will be erased as soon as possible, but definitely not later than one year after the date of the recording.

TO BE COMPLETED BY THE PATIENT (delete as appropriate)

I have read and understood the information leaflet.

I give my permission for my consultation to be video-recorded.
I do not give my permission for my consultation to be video-recorded.

State here if you wish to limit the use to which the tape might be put, and whether you require the tape to be erased within a specified period of time.

....

Signature of patient **before consultation:**

....Date ....

Signature of person accompanying patient:

....Date ....

Following my consultation I am still willing/I no longer wish for my consultation to be used for the above purposes.

Signature of person **after consultation:**

....Date ....

Signature of person accompanying patient:

....Date ....

Appendix 2

CSQ and scoring instructions

CSQ   CONFIDENTIAL

Eli Lilly National Clinical Audit Centre
Department of General Practice and Primary Health Care
University of Leicester

CONSULTATION SATISFACTION QUESTIONNAIRE

This form contains a list of questions. They ask you what you think of your last visit to the doctor. Please answer all the questions. Your answers will be kept entirely confidential and will not be shown to the doctor, so feel free to say what you wish. Please do not write your name on the form and be sure to place this form in the box provided before you leave today.

Some of the questions will appear similar. This is deliberate and is necessary to make sure they are reliable. Please answer them all. **For each question circle the answer that is closest to what you think.** 'Neutral' means you have no feelings either way.

For example:

'This doctor was bored'   Strongly agree / Agree / Neutral / Disagree / Strongly disagree

1	I am totally satisfied with my visit to this doctor	Strongly agree / Agree / Neutral / Disagree / Strongly disagree
2	This doctor was very careful to check everything when examining me	Strongly agree / Agree / Neutral / Disagree / Strongly disagree
3	I will follow this doctor's advice because I think he/she is absolutely right	Strongly agree / Agree / Neutral / Disagree / Strongly disagree
4	I felt able to tell this doctor about very personal things	Strongly agree / Agree / Neutral / Disagree / Strongly disagree
5	The time I was able to spend with the doctor was a bit too short	Strongly agree / Agree / Neutral / Disagree / Strongly disagree
6	This doctor told me everything about my treatment	Strongly agree / Agree / Neutral / Disagree / Strongly disagree
7	Some things about my consultation with the doctor could have been better	Strongly agree / Agree / Neutral / Disagree / Strongly disagree

Reproduced by kind permission of Professor Richard Baker, Director of the Clinical Governance Unit, University of Leicester, from Baker RH (1990) Development of a questionnaire to assess patients' satisfaction with consultations in general practice. *Br J Gen Pract*. **40**: 487–90.

8	There are some things this doctor does not know about me	Strongly agree / Agree / Neutral / Disagree / Strongly disagree
9	This doctor examined me very thoroughly	Strongly agree / Agree / Neutral / Disagree / Strongly disagree
10	I thought this doctor took notice of me as a person	Strongly agree / Agree / Neutral / Disagree / Strongly disagree
11	The time I was allowed to spend with the doctor was not long enough to deal with everything I wanted	Strongly agree / Agree / Neutral / Disagree / Strongly disagree
12	I understand my illness much better after seeing this doctor	Strongly agree / Agree / Neutral / Disagree / Strongly disagree
13	This doctor was interested in me as a person not just my illness	Strongly agree / Agree / Neutral / Disagree / Strongly disagree
14	This doctor knows all about me	Strongly agree / Agree / Neutral / Disagree / Strongly disagree
15	I felt this doctor really knew what I was thinking	Strongly agree / Agree / Neutral / Disagree / Strongly disagree
16	I wish it had been possible to spend a little longer with the doctor	Strongly agree / Agree / Neutral / Disagree / Strongly disagree
17	I am not completely satisfied with my visit to the doctor	Strongly agree / Agree / Neutral / Disagree / Strongly disagree
18	I would find it difficult to tell this doctor about some private things	Strongly agree / Agree / Neutral / Disagree / Strongly disagree

How old are you? _____ years

Are you male? _____ Or female? _____ (Tick which applies)

Do you have any other comments about the consultation? _____

_____

_____

THANK YOU FOR COMPLETING THIS QUESTIONNAIRE

Calculating Satisfaction Scores

Description

Details of how the Satisfaction Scores are calculated are given here. The EPi Info program we provide uses these formulae. You can, of course, calculate the Satisfaction Scores without using Epi Info and use them in ways other than those we suggest. Be imaginative!

Instructions

The statements on the SSQ and CSQ are not all worded in the same direction, so that it is possible for 'Strongly agree' to indicate satisfaction in some questions (e.g. SSQ question 1) and dissatisfaction in others (e.g. SSQ question 10). The calculation of satisfaction takes this into account.

After scoring for each question Strongly agree = 1, Agree = 2, Neutral = 3, Disagree = 4 or Strongly disagree = 5, then subtract the positive question scores from 6, so the higher the score the greater the satisfaction. Add together the scores from the questions for each aspect and convert to a percentage of the highest possible score from that aspect – that is, 5 times the number of questions. This now gives a value between 20 and 100, which is converted to a 0 to 100 scale by multiplying by 5/4 (= 1.25) and then subtracting 25.

The analysis given here handles missing data values (unanswered questions) by omitting those questionnaires from the relevant calculations.

The questions relating to each aspect are shown in the table below, and the formulae are then given.

Questions	Positive	Negative
General satisfaction	1	7, 17
Professional care	2, 3, 6, 9, 10, 12, 13	
Depth of relationship	4, 14 , 15	8, 18
Perceived time		5, 11, 16

The formulae for calculating the scores are as follows.

General satisfaction $= [((6-Q1 + Q7 + Q17) * 100 / (5*3)] * 1.25 - 25$

Professional care $= [((6-Q2) + (6-Q3) + (6-Q6) + (6-Q9) + (6-Q10) + (6-Q12) + (6-Q13) * 100 / (5*7)] * 1.25 - 25$

Depth of relationship $= [((6-Q4) + Q8 + (6-Q14) + (6-Q15) + Q18) * 100 / (5*5)] * 1.25 - 25$

Perceived time $[(Q5 + Q11 + Q16) * 100 / (5*3)] * 1.25 - 25$

Index